CHRIS KILLIP

The Tate Photography Series is a celebration of photography by artists in the Tate collection, presenting some of the most significant photographers in the world today. Each book focuses on an individual photographer and includes a specially selected sequence of images and an introduction by a Tate curator, alongside a conversation about each photographer's practice. These collaborations between artists and experts serve to enrich our understanding of photography and its connection to everyday life.

Each year the Tate Photography Series adopts a unifying theme across four books that addresses social, political and cultural issues of our time. The theme for Series Two is Ecology and Environment, featuring photographers who examine aspects of our relationship with the natural world, environment and changing climate.

While overwhelming hard scientific evidence seems all too easy to dispute and ignore, artistic approaches to considering our place in the world appear to be a more effective way to reconnect and change. Photographic artists, ever-curious, sensitive and attuned to noticing patterns, creatively document and mediate reality to help us see.

This series explores Richard Mosse's work in the Amazon rainforest, finding new ways to represent climate change; Chris Killip's *Seacoal* series in North-East England, where a community subsists on discarded fossil fuel; Lieko Shiga's series *Spiral Shore*, which documents and reimagines a coastal community in Japan's Miyagi Prefecture that was struck by the earthquake and tsunami of 2011; and Claudia Andujar's life work protecting the Yanomami, one of Brazil's largest indigenous groups.

Series Two

2:1   **CLAUDIA ANDUJAR**
2:2   **CHRIS KILLIP**
2:3   **RICHARD MOSSE**
2:4   **LIEKO SHIGA**

CHRIS KILLIP

Edited by
Bilal Akkouche

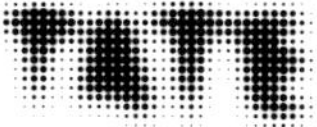

First published 2023 by order of the Tate Trustees
by Tate Publishing, a division of Tate Enterprises Ltd,
Millbank, London SW1P 4RG
www.tate.org.uk/publishing

A catalogue record for this book is available from
the British Library

ISBN 978 1 84976 867 2

Distributed in the United States and Canada
by ABRAMS, New York

Library of Congress Control Number applied for

Series Editors: Simon Armstrong and
Yasufumi Nakamori
Senior Editor: Nicola Bion
Production: Bill Jones
Picture Research: Emma O'Neill
Designed by Sarah Boris
Colour reproduction by Westerham Press, London
Printed and bound in the UK by Westerham Press,
London

Front cover: *Brian in a duffle coat* 1984
Back cover top: *Blackie and Matty* 1982
Back cover bottom: *Man resting and spotted horse,
Seacoal Beach* 1984

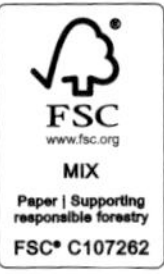

CONTENTS

INTRODUCTION

This publication focuses on the themes of ecology and the environment through the photographic practice of Chris Killip by showcasing two series: *Seacoal* (1982–4) and *Skinningrove* (1982–4). Alongside this, it seeks to contextualise the communities of Lynemouth and Skinningrove within the extremely precarious post-industrial Britain. The text also interrogates the way in which Killip was able to access both communities, and his desire to highlight their humanity and their dependence on the natural environment for their food and income.

Killip's *Seacoal* series documents the extreme conditions of work felt by Lynemouth's seacoal community who, in order to survive, fished out coal from the sea that had been discarded by those working in the coal mine and power station nearby. In *Skinningrove*, Killip captures the fishing community within the North Yorkshire coastal village setting. These intimate works depict the community's relationship to the environment, as Killip recalled, 'Skinningrove fishermen believed that the sea in front of them was their private territory, theirs alone.'[1] By comparing the two series, this publication illustrates the intrinsic link between the community and the environment, and the ways in which they coexist.

Chris Killip was born in Douglas, Isle of Man, in 1946. He left school at the age of sixteen and in 1964 decided to pursue a career in photography. In 1975 Killip moved to Newcastle upon Tyne on a two-year fellowship as the Northern Arts Photography Fellow. During his time in Newcastle he was a founding member, exhibition curator and adviser of the Side Gallery, as well as its director, from 1977 to 1979. Throughout his time in the north-east of England, he created several photographic series including *Skinningrove* (1982–4), *Seacoal* (1982–4) and *The Station* (1981–5). Many photographs from these series were featured in what is often cited as the most important photographic book on England in the 1980s, *In Flagrante* (1988), winner of the Henri

Cartier-Bresson Award, which sought to document the devastating impact of deindustrialisation on working-class communities in northern England: 'I wanted to record people's lives because I valued them. I wanted them to be remembered. If you take a photograph of someone they are immortalised, they're there forever. For me that was important, that you're acknowledging people's lives, and also contextualising people's lives.'[2]

In 1991 Killip moved to the USA having been given a position at the Department of Visual and Environmental Studies, Harvard University, as a Visiting Lecturer. He was then made a tenured professor in 1994 and became department chair from 1994 to 1998. From then on, he acted as a Professor of Visual and Environmental Studies until his retirement in 2017. Killip continued to live in Cambridge, Massachusetts, until his death in October 2020, aged seventy-four. His legacy as one of the most influential British photographers of his generation continues to this day.

Killip's work has been included in several displays and exhibitions throughout Britain and internationally, including the *After Industry: Communities in North England 1960s–1980s* collection display at Tate Britain, London (2021–2); *Chris Killip, retrospective*, The Photographers' Gallery, London (2022–3); *20/20: Chris Killip / Graham Smith*, Augusta Edwards Fine Art, London (2022); *The Station*, Martin Parr Foundation, Bristol (2020); *The Last Ships*, Laing Art Gallery, Newcastle (2018); *Now Then: Chris Killip and the Making of In Flagrante*, J. Paul Getty Museum, Los Angeles (2017); *Isle of Man Revisited*, Manx Museum, Isle of Man (2016); and *Chris Killip – 75 Photographs*, Tate Britain, London (2014).

Killip's work also features in the permanent collections of major institutions including the Museum of Modern Art, New York; George Eastman House, Rochester, NY; Fine Arts Museums of San Francisco; Museum Folkwang, Essen; Stedelijk Museum, Amsterdam; National Gallery of Australia, Canberra; Tate, London; and the Victoria and Albert Museum, London.

Bilal Akkouche
Assistant Curator, International Art, Tate

1   *Chris Killip: Skinningrove*, Göttingen 2022.
2   Diane Smyth, 'Now Then: Chris Killip and the Making of In Flagrante', *British Journal of Photography*, 6 June 2017, https://www.1854.photography/2017/06/now-then-chris-killip-and-the-making-of-in-flagrante/, accessed 11 May 2023.

CHRIS KILLIP
1946–2020

The villages of Lynemouth in Northumberland and Skinningrove in
North Yorkshire acted as sites of representation for Chris Killip to
document the lives of those struggling to survive within the context
of the deindustrialisation of Britain. Killip's two bodies of work,
Seacoal (1982–4) photographed in Lynemouth and *Skinningrove*
(1982–4) shot in the village of Skinningrove, make up part of his
wider documentation of the decline of heavy industry – steelworks,
shipyards and coalmines – in his famous book *In Flagrante* (1988),
which he describes as a 'portrait of working class struggles at that
time'.[1] Photographed against the backdrop of the miners' strikes, the
Seacoal and *Skinningrove* works illustrate the ways in which those on
the fringes of society had to utilise the environment in order to survive.

Taken at Lynemouth, a once important colliery village, fifteen
miles north of Newcastle upon Tyne, Killip produced the *Seacoal*
photographs between 1983 and 1984.[2] He recalled the site as follows:
'The beach beneath me was full of activity with horses and carts
backed into the sea. Men were standing in the sea next to the carts,
using small wire nets attached to poles to fish out the coal from the
water beneath them. The place confounded time; here the Middle
Ages and the twentieth century intertwined.'[3]

The techniques employed by the seacoalers caught Killip's eye and he
described the strange sight of the coal floats: wire mesh nets used to
capture the coal from the sea.[4] Seventy of the *Seacoal* photographs
were first exhibited at the Side Gallery in Newcastle, and twelve prints
from the series were included in an exhibition along with works by
photographer Graham Smith, *Another Country*, held at the Serpentine

Gallery, London, in 1985.[5] Immersing himself in a small working-class community in Skinningrove, Killip photographed the community's attempt to create a substitutive economy around inshore fishing following the closure of a local iron and steel plant.[6] The photographs in both *Seacoal* and *Skinningrove* illustrate the adaptations such communities were forced to make within the British landscape and how they utilised the environment to navigate their newfound precariousness. The horses and carts that seemed 'so 19th century', employed because Lynemouth beach was too soft for motor vehicles[7], are an example of this.

It is important to reflect on the fraught context within which Killip was working. The 1970s and 1980s were a time in which the country's three main heavy industries suffered.[8] The miners' strike from March 1984 to March 1985, otherwise known as the Great Coal Strike, peaked with the Battle of Orgreave in which thousands of protestors were met by a charge of horse-mounted police in full riot gear.[9] Prior to creating the *Seacoal* series, Killip stopped working on his own projects to photograph the strikes, which culminated in around 5,000 photographs documenting the strikes in the north-east of England.[10] According to Haworth-Booth, Killip's decision to donate the material to the local branch of the National Union of Mineworkers demonstrated his solidarity with those on strike. Unemployment in the north-east in the 1980s was at its highest since the Great Depression and the local coastal communities had to balance rebellion against the state with the need to fish for survival.[11]

> Since Mrs Thatcher was first voted into office the number of people living below even the official poverty lines has doubled. They now number about 12 million. By contrast, during the last four years, the number of millionaires in the country has risen from 7,000 to 20,000. In the North-East it is estimated that there are 1,500 deaths a year due to exposure or starvation. The infamous distinction between the South and North is not one between wealth and poverty but between the safe-guarded and the abandoned.[12]

Killip's photobook, *In Flagrante*, is often considered one of the most important publications on the topic of 1980s Britain. The phrase 'in flagrante' means 'caught in the act', and Killip suggests that 'you can see me in the shadow, but I'm trying to undermine your confidence in what you're seeing, to remind people that photographs are a construction, a fabrication. They were made by somebody. They are not to be trusted. It's as simple as that.'[13] According to Clive Dilnot, *In Flagrante* should be read as a savage critique of Thatcherism as it covers fifteen years of industrial decline, and does not containing a single picture of wage work.[14] In describing *In Flagrante*, Killip posited that: 'This is a subjective book about my time in England. I take what isn't mine and I covet other people's lives. The photographs can tell you more about me than about what they describe. The book is a fiction about metaphor.'[15]

In order to gain access to the communities of Lynemouth and Skinningrove during such a culturally, politically and economically divisive period, Killip had to embed himself within their environments and demonstrate that his interest in documenting them was sincere. After being violently chased off the beach on his first day of visiting and photographing Lynemouth, Killip's attempts to root himself within the community took around seven years.[16] Once the trust had been gained, Killip lived in a caravan on the beach for more than a year, becoming 'very famous for making cups of tea, and people used to come. It was like my studio, really. People would sit down and the entrance fee to my place was I'd be photographing you.'[17]

Through this use of the caravan, Killip was able to capture the morning celebrations as the men returned from horse races, children playing and working among the coal, and families huddled around communal fires. Storms that threatened to overturn the caravan contrasted with dawns of perishing stillness,[18] resulting in a body of work that serves as a testament to the human relationship with the elements. Speaking about his photograph *Rocker and his Toad, Seacoal Camp* 1983, Killip said that a young Rocker was 'explaining to me the difference between a frog and a toad ... When I first met Rocker, he was about seven years old. I spent about three years on and off watching him grow, but I then stayed in touch with the family when I wasn't photographing there anymore. I like keeping in contact with people.'[19] The artist's persistence and acknowledgement of the need to embed himself within the community of Lynemouth beach led to a series of works that showcase profound humanity on the fringes of society.

Similarly, the works made in Skinningrove came about during a period in which Killip lived near the village on the outskirts of Newcastle. Fully immersed in the small fishing community, he built relationships with many of the individuals, including a young man named Bever whom Killip captured enjoying the early morning sunlight following his release from prison:

He had been locked up for a month, I think. And he had walked
into the village, and I think he had walked quite a long way. And
it was about just before six in the morning, and he came back to
Skinningrove and he is just taking in the sun. It was the first sun
he had seen in a bit and it was the sun coming up in the morning.
And I am talking to him and photographing him, but I could do that
because I knew him. He had been in a pub fight a month before
and a policeman had come towards him, and he drew out his
nightstick and Bever looked at it and he punched him right on the
jaw apparently and of course, Bever is very big and strong and he
knocked the policeman out. And he knocked the policeman out.
And as a consequence, he had to be locked up for four weeks. He is
not a bad fella; it was just circumstance ... Maybe he shouldn't have
hit him so hard![20]

Killip's proximity to the people he photographed comes across in both
bodies of work. The sincere depictions of everyday life on the fringes
of society, alongside his recollections of the characters photographed,
illustrate his commitment to becoming part of the community he
sought to platform. His account of Bever's interaction with the police,
together with the photograph *Bever taking in the early morning sun*
1982, demonstrates his desire to uplift those who were forgotten
by a society that did not care about their needs or desires. Killip's
documentation of this interaction between humanity and the state
centres their experience and readers are left questioning their own
preconceived ideas.

Killip's desire to showcase the very essence of humanity in a context of
adversity resulted in photographs that portray joy as well as a sense of
purpose. Take, for example, the pictures of *Rocker and John dressed
in fertilizer sacks* 1983 or even *Helen Laidler with her parents Brian
and Rosie and her sister Alison* 1983. Here, joy permeates as children
play among the coal washed up on the Lynemouth coastline: 'there
was lots of energy and lots of fun... there was rivalry and enthusiasms
and passions' ... 'people were not despairing.'[21] His memory of
the seacoalers illustrates his desire to become one of them while
photographing them. It is clear this would not have been possible if
he had not sought to embed himself within the community. Killip's
closeness to the seacoalers is well documented and reflected in his
own recollections:

Looking at these pictures again [*Seacoal* series] I see this place
differently, and maybe more clearly. The children look so beautiful.

At the time they were just there, the children I knew, who were like the place, full of life. I cherish the great friendships I made. The generosity of Brian and Rosie Laidler, who always wanted to feed me, even when money was tight. The ongoing, undecided arguments between Trevor and Brian over whether pigs could get sunburnt. The illegal trotting races for big money against the 'Townies', which took place at dawn on the main road. The morning I slipped at one such race and my flash went off as I fell to the ground. Hannibal Harker, who didn't know me, picked up a scaffolding pole to brain me, until Trevor put a hand up to stop him with the immortal words 'Hannibal, it's OK, he's with us'. And there was Tommy, who was always suspecting I was a sleeper, a plant who had been sent to garner evidence for some unknown future use. I used to be very indignant about his suspicions, although I realize now that this may have come true, but in a different way than either of us could have imagined.[22]

Both the *Seacoal* and *Skinningrove* series make clear the intrinsic link between humans and the environment and ecology. The communities of Lynemouth and Skinningrove were reliant on the coastline for their food and income. The Ellington Colliery close to Lynemouth was active until 2005, and for almost a century coal had been deposited on the beach. Ex-miners and a small community of travellers moved to the beach to eke out a precarious living from harvesting the coal on the tides or retrieving it from the beach itself.[23] The coal was only able to be retrieved due to the separation from the waste in the sea. The coal floated while the waste sunk, and then the tide brought the coal in closer to the coastline. The seacoalers were reliant on the natural environment for this separation to take place and for the coal to be washed up on the shore. According to Haworth-Booth, around forty to fifty people earned a living on Lynemouth beach, selling the coal for a pound per cartload, which was in turn sold to a coal factor that owned the beach and was a licensed distributor to the National Coal Board.[24]

The coastal village of Skinningrove was also a place where the sea provided a substitute economy around inshore fishing, after mass redundancy in the north-east. People took great risks to make a living in this precarious economic environment, and the fishing boats were in very poor condition. Killip reflected:

I often wondered why I was in Skinningrove. You don't know what's going to happen, and for better or worse, a photograph is a chronicle of a death foretold. It's the one thing about everybody that you do know. They are going to die. You don't know when or how. But things happen. And you hope when you photograph, you do it well, and that they're well-remembered.[25]

Both communities were helped by, but also at the mercy of, their local environment. Ultimately, the *Seacoal* and *Skinningrove* series showcase the difficulties of living on the fringes of society during the Thatcher era, but also illustrate the ways in which communities faced adversity head on. Killip's pictures granted the individuals agency by depicting the joy felt by the children and the sense of purpose the young adults had in forging a living from retrieving the coal at Lynemouth beach or fishing in the Skinningrove sea. His recollections demonstrate how embedded he became and his deep affection for the plight of the communities, which can be seen in each of the photographs in the series. Reflecting upon his time with the seacoalers, Killip recounted:

> The seacoal camp has been levelled and landscaped. The coalmine is gone and with it the coal. All that is left is a small council-approved caravan site for Travellers. Trevor moved away and we eventually lost touch. I remain close to the Laidler family who now live in a house forty miles from the old camp. Brian and Rosie's grandchildren are now older than their children were when I took the photographs which are in this book.
>
> I have never again met anyone quite like Brian. He's hard to describe. Dickensian is the word that most comes to mind. One day I was walking along the beach with him when, completely out of the blue, he stopped and asked me 'Do you know the commandment, love one another?' I replied, 'Yes, I do.' 'It's not a bad idea, is it Chris?' and we carried on walking.[26]

Bilal Akkouche

1   Laura Hubber, 'Caught in the Act: A Conversation with Photographer Chris Killip', *Getty*, 7 July 2017, https://blogs.getty.edu/iris/caught-in-the-act-a-conversation-with-photographer-chris-killip/, accessed 5 May 2023.
2   Mark Haworth-Booth, 'Chris Killip: Scenes from Another Country', *Aperture*, Summer 1986, p.16.
3   Chris Killip, *Seacoal*, Göttingen 2011, p.17.
4   Carolina A. Miranda, 'Seven Photos, Seven Stories: Chris Killip on Capturing the Declining Industrial Towns of England in the '70s and '80s', *Los Angeles Times*, 21 July 2017, https://www.latimes.com/entertainment/arts/la-et-cam-chris-killip-getty-museum-20170721-htmlstory.html, accessed 5 May 2023.
5   Mark Haworth-Booth, 'Chris Killip: Scenes from Another Country', p.16.
6   Clive Dilnot, 'Chris Killip: The Last Photographer of the Working Class', *Afterimage*, vol.39, May–June 2012, p.17.
7   Quote from Chris Killip, taken from Carolina A. Miranda, 'Seven Photos, Seven Stories'.
8   Laura Hubber, 'Caught in the Act'.
9   Mark Haworth-Booth, 'Chris Killip: Scenes from Another Country', p.17.
10   Ibid.
11   Ken Grant, 'Edgelands', in Ken Grant (ed.), *Chris Killip*, London 2022, p.79.
12   John Berger and Sylvia Grant, '[Walking Back Home]', in Chris Killip, *In Flagrante*, London 1988, p.87.
13   Laura Hubber, 'Caught in the Act'.
14   Clive Dilnot, 'Chris Killip: The Last Photographer of the Working Class', p.15.
15   Chris Killip, *In Flagrante*, London 1988, p.1.
16   Clive Dilnot, 'Chris Killip: The Last Photographer of the Working Class', p.17.
17   Laura Hubber, 'Caught in the Act'.
18   Ken Grant, 'Edgelands', p.81.
19   Laura Hubber, 'Caught in the Act'.
20   Ibid.
21   Quote from Chris Killip, taken from Carolina A. Miranda, 'Seven Photos, Seven Stories'.
22   Chris Killip, *Seacoal*, Göttingen 2011, p.3.
23   Clive Dilnot, 'Chris Killip: The Last Photographer of the Working Class', p.17.
24   Mark Haworth-Booth, 'Chris Killip: Scenes from Another Country', p.20.
25   Laura Hubber, 'Caught in the Act'.
26   Chris Killip, *Seacoal*, Göttingen 2011, p.3.

PLATES

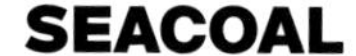

SEACOAL

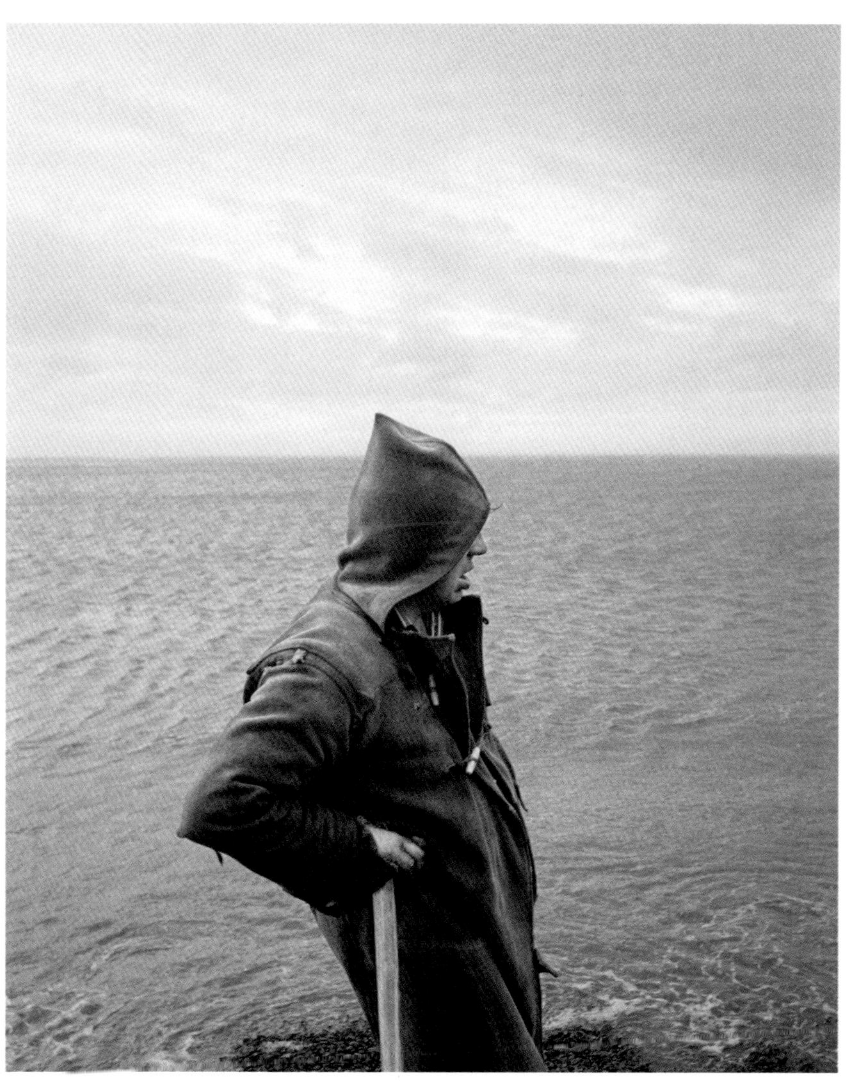

     Brian in a duffle coat 1984

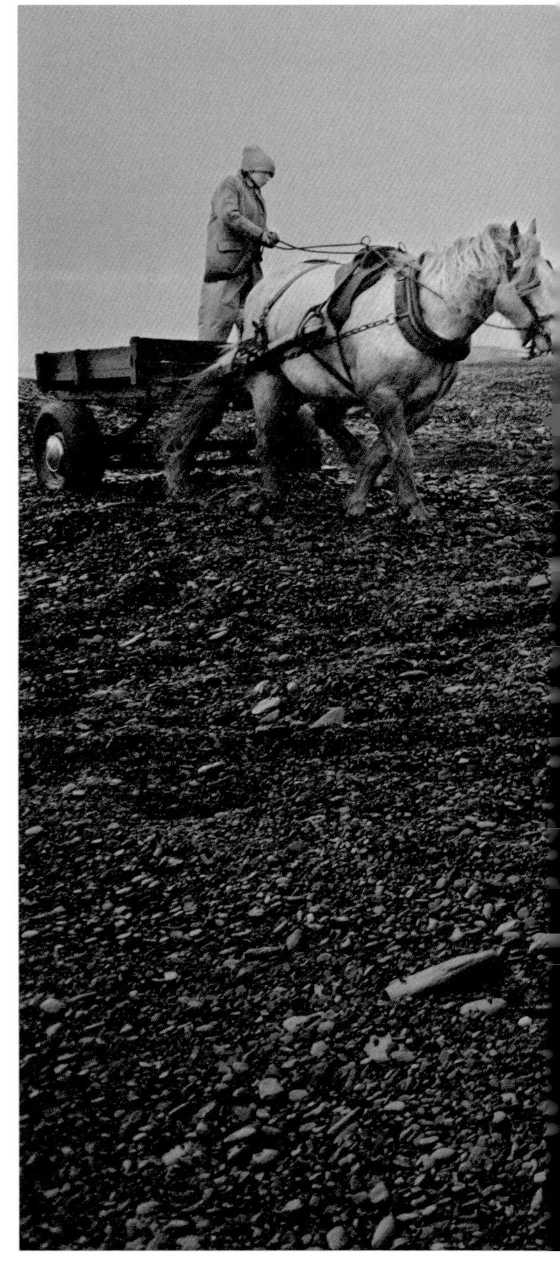

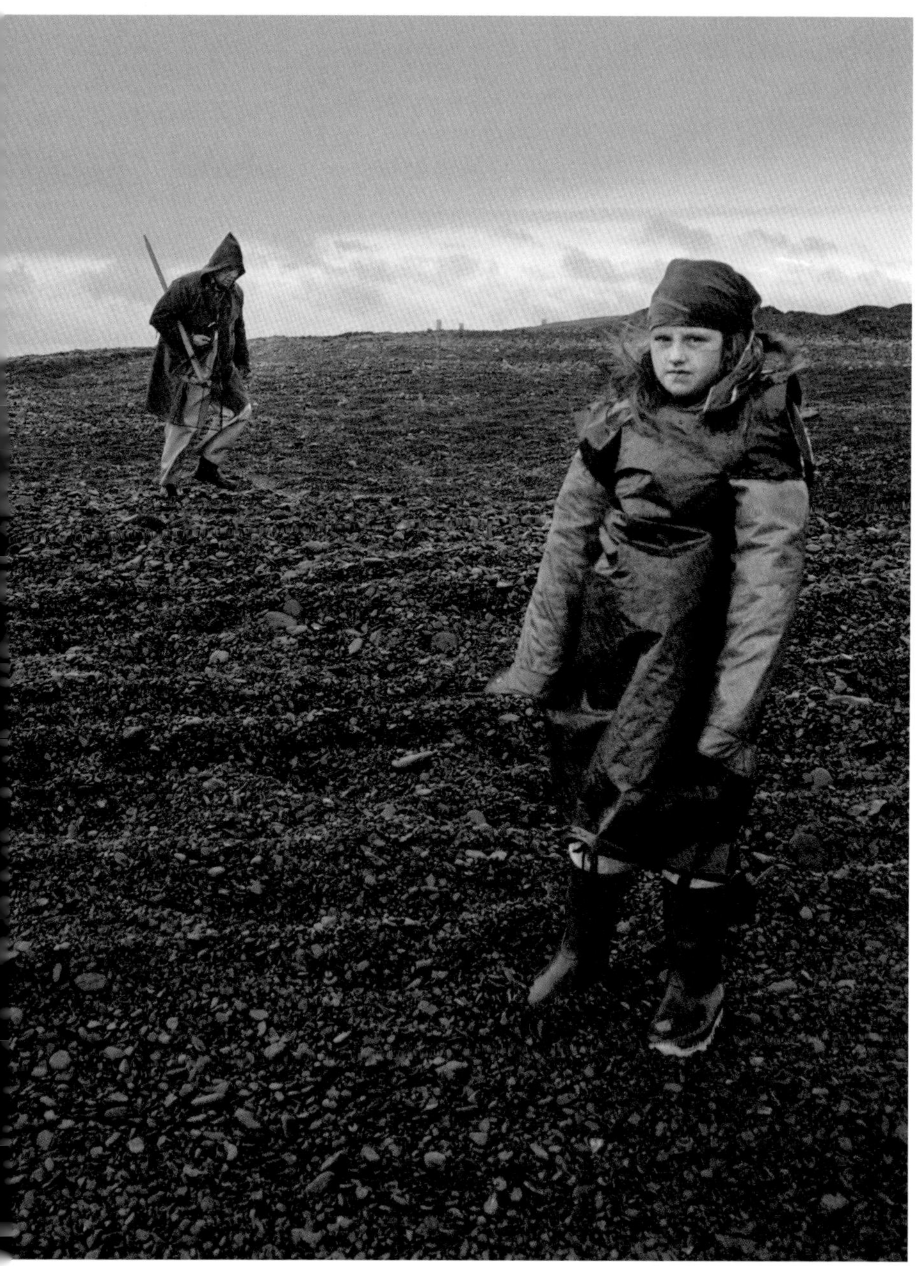

    Alison, Brian and Claire on the beach 1983

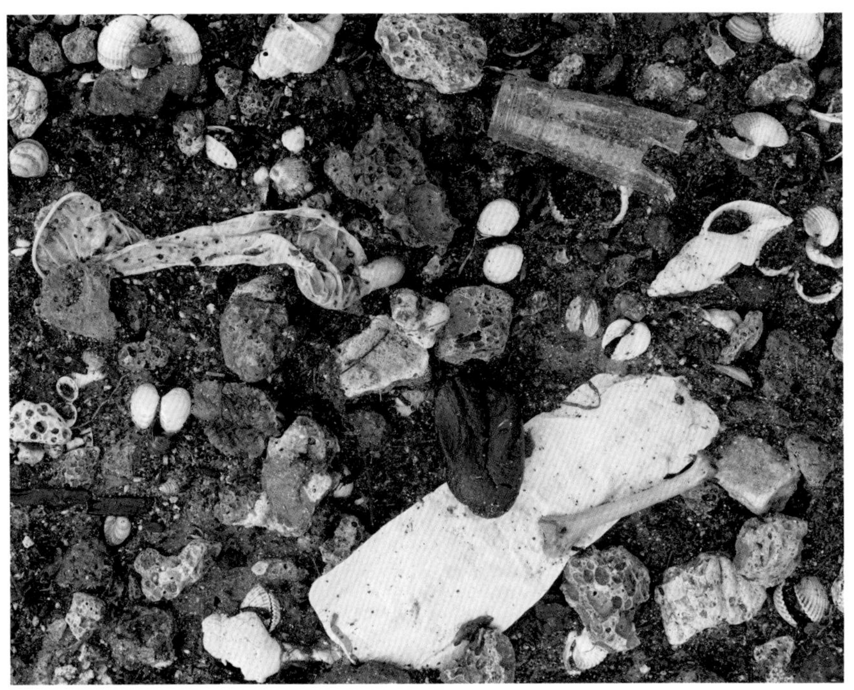

    Beach, Askam-in-Furness, Cumbria 1982

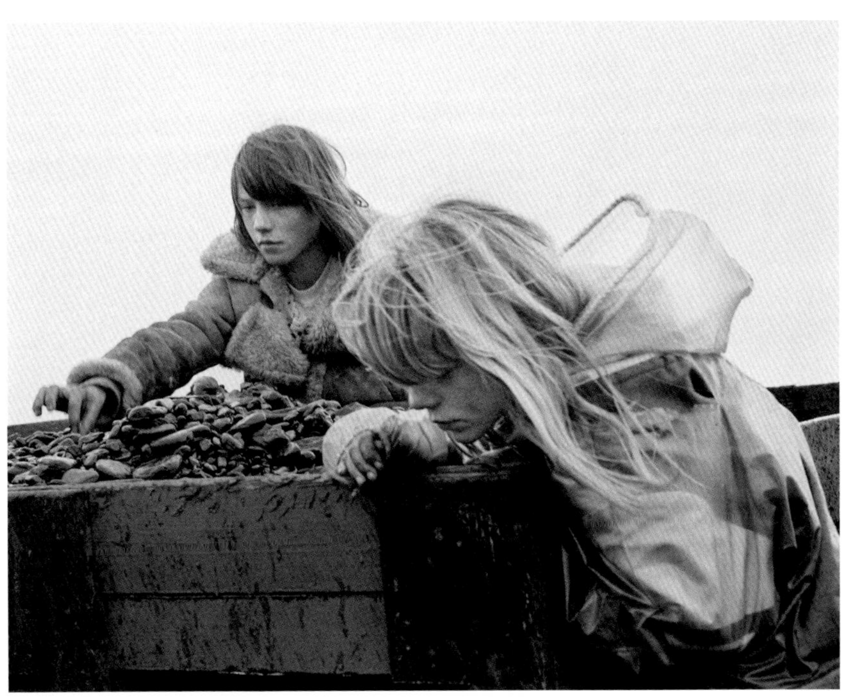

 Nini and Helen picking out stones from the cart 1983

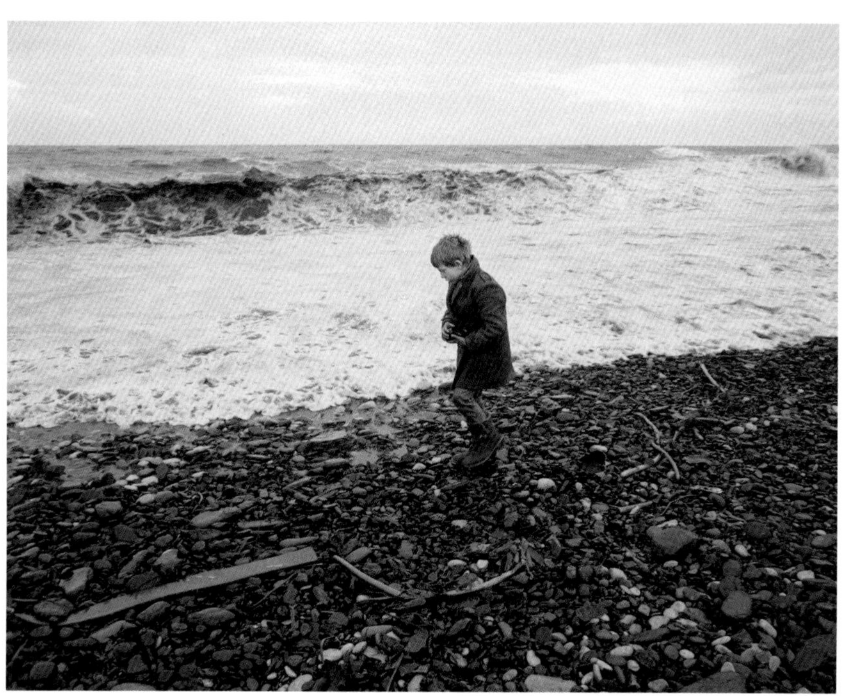

 Rocker hand-picking seacoal 1984

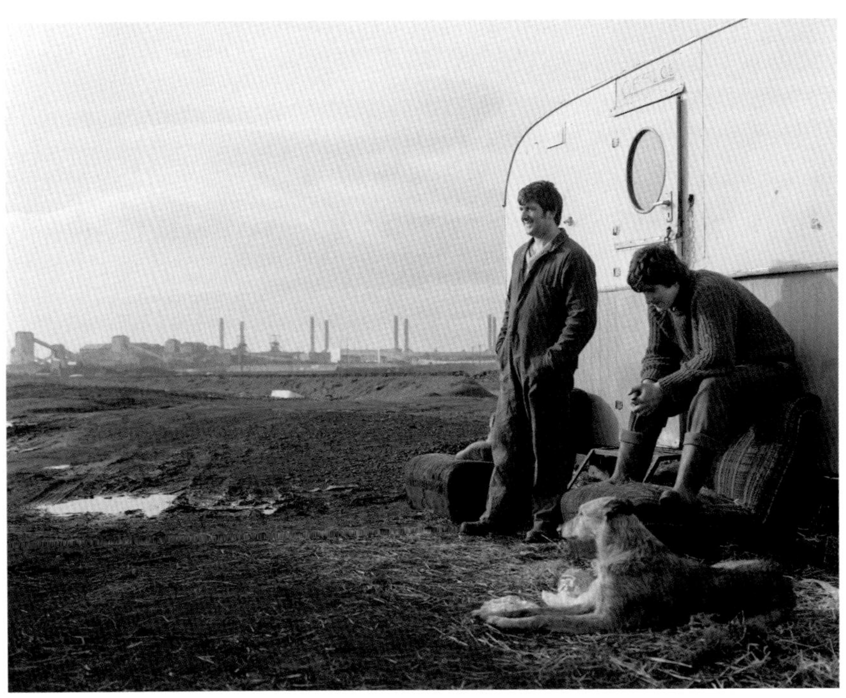

 'Critch' and Sean surveying the landscape, Seacoal Camp, Lynemouth, Northumberland 1982

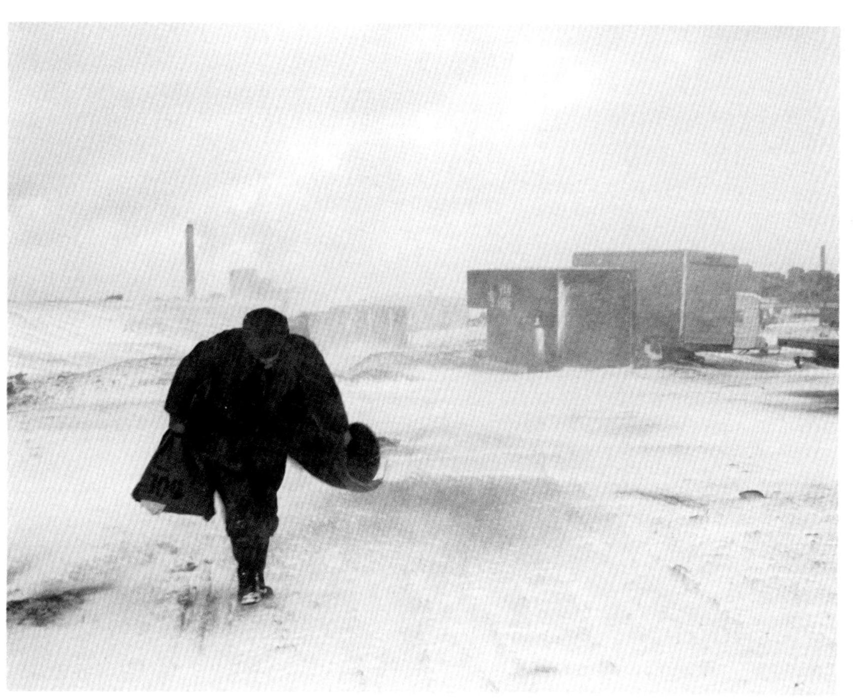

 Cookie in the Snow, Seacoal Camp, Lynemouth, Northumberland 1984

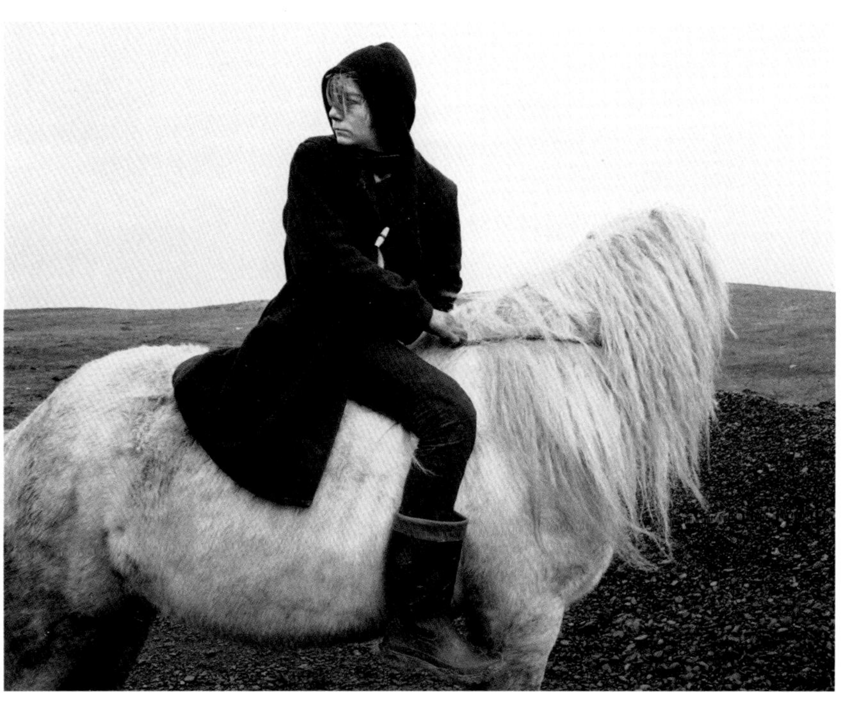

    Boo on a horse 1984

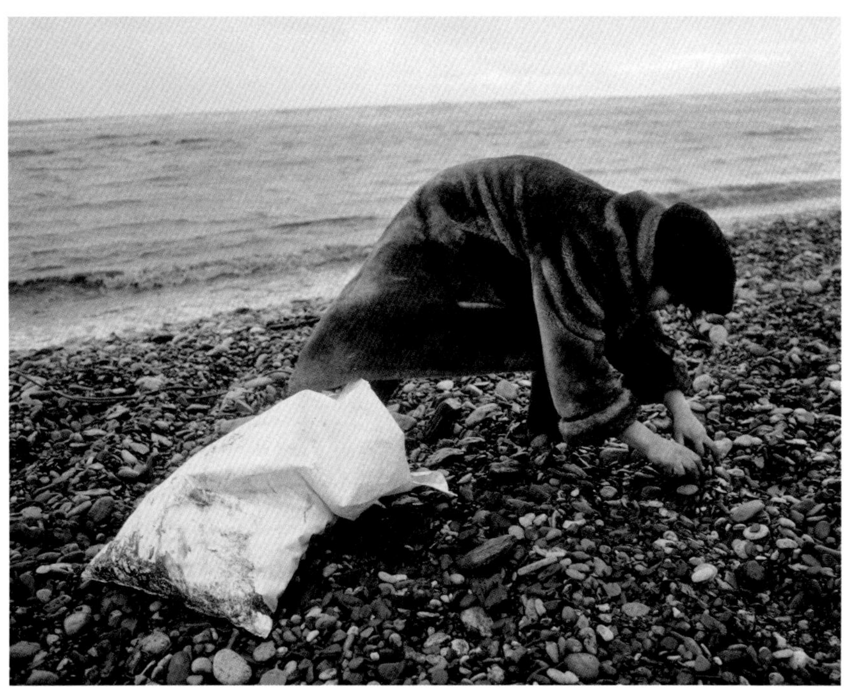

    Moira hand-picking in the very good fur coat 1984

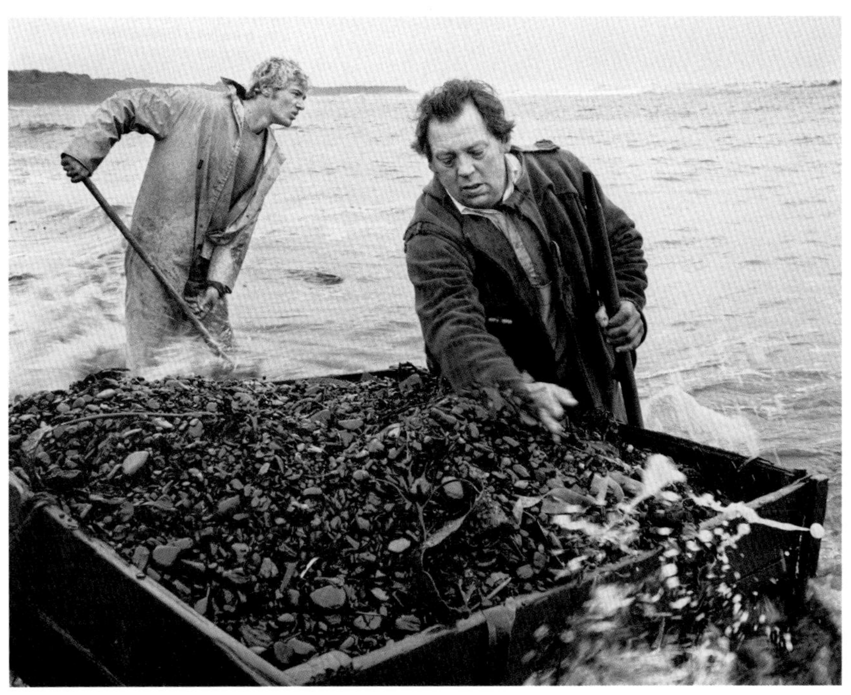

 Brian and unidentified man in the water 1984

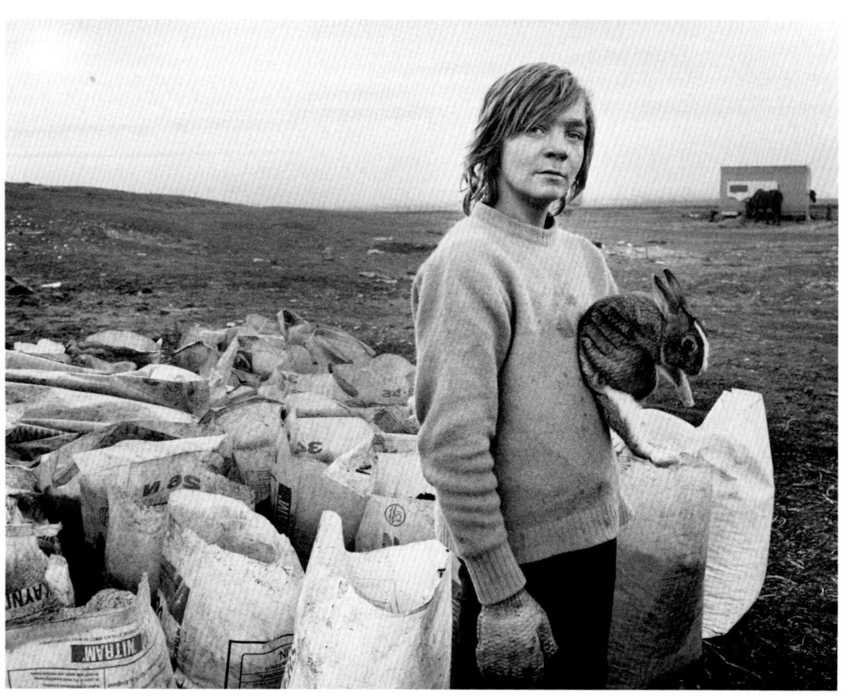

          Boo and his rabbit 1984

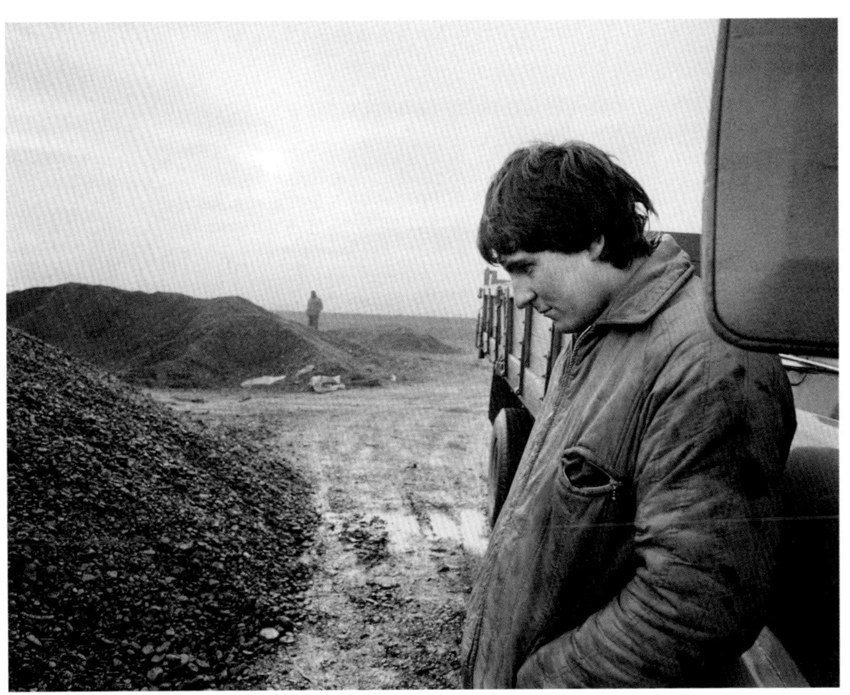

     Sean leaning against his truck 1983

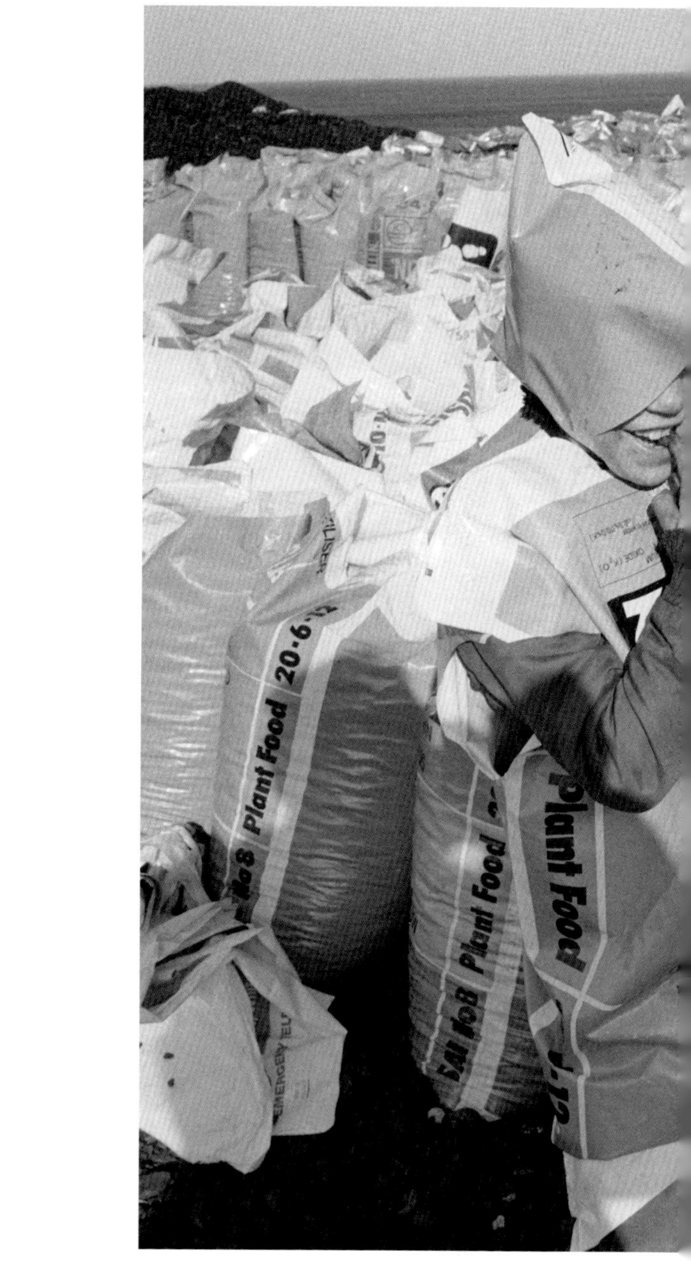

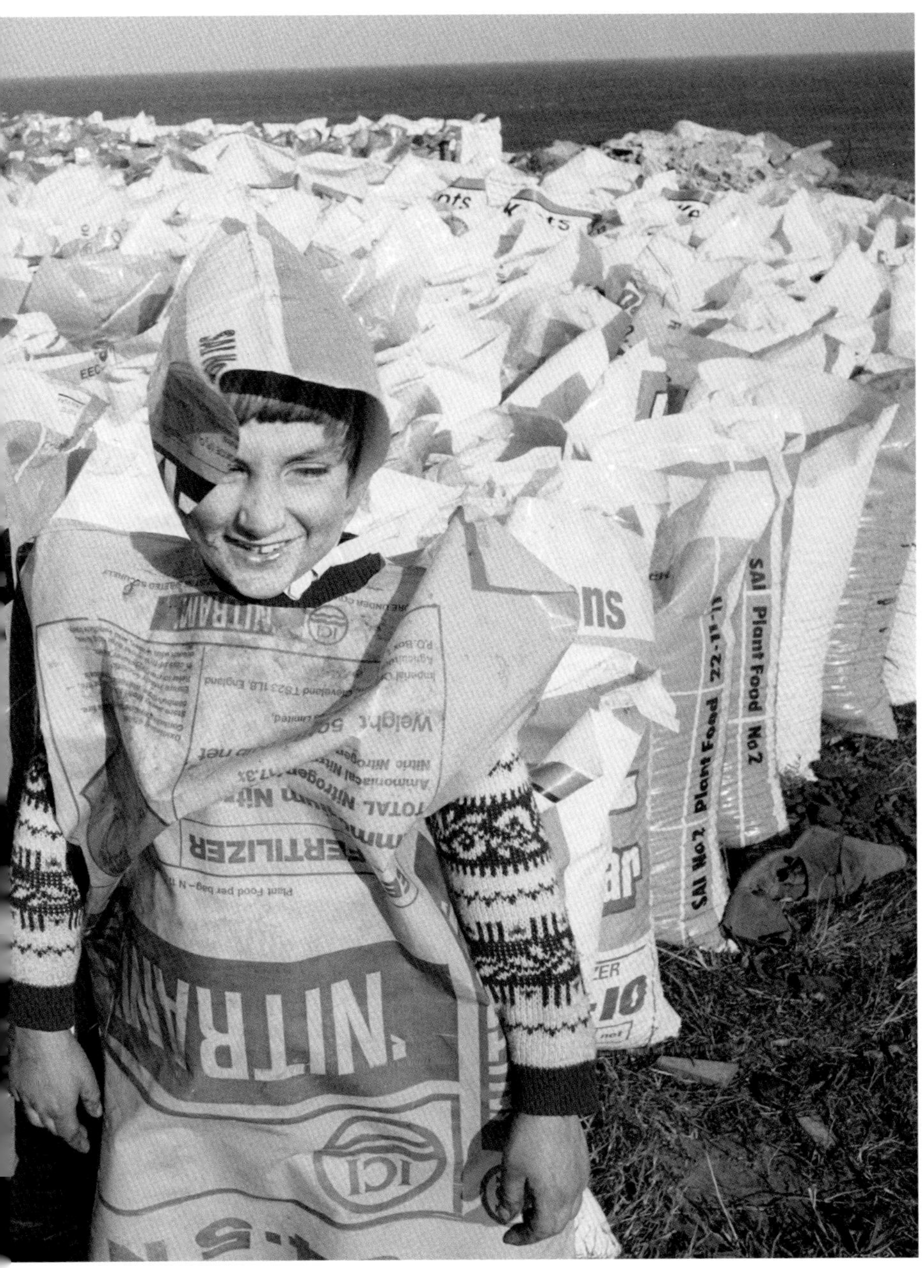

     Rocker and John dressed in fertilizer sacks 1983

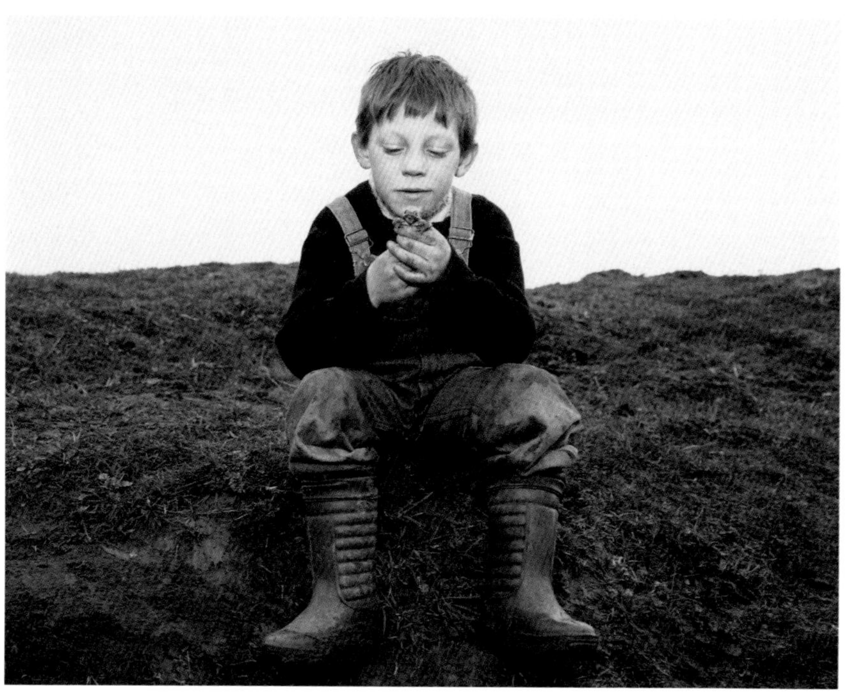

     Rocker and his Toad, Seacoal Camp 1983

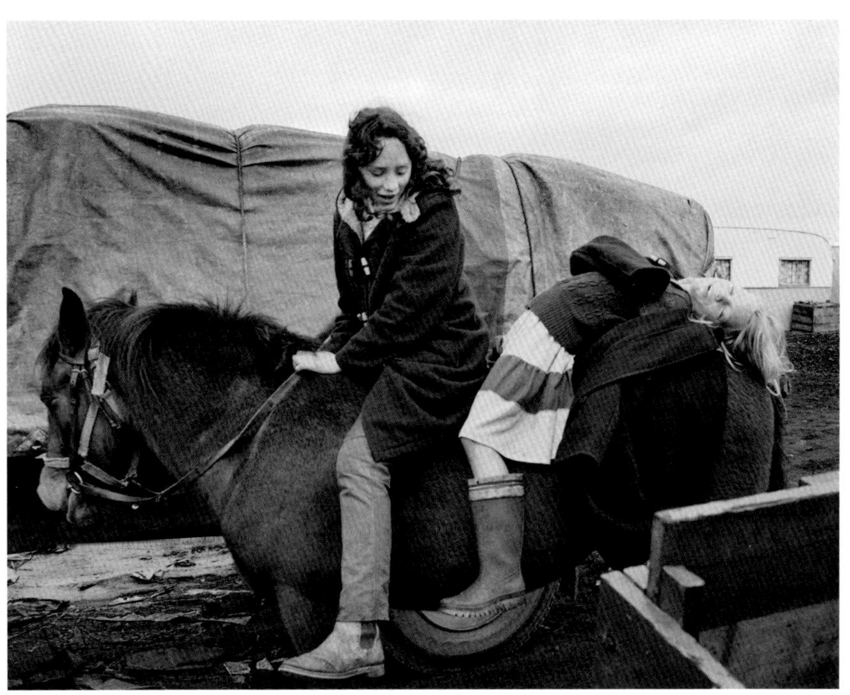

  Alison and Helen on a horse 1983

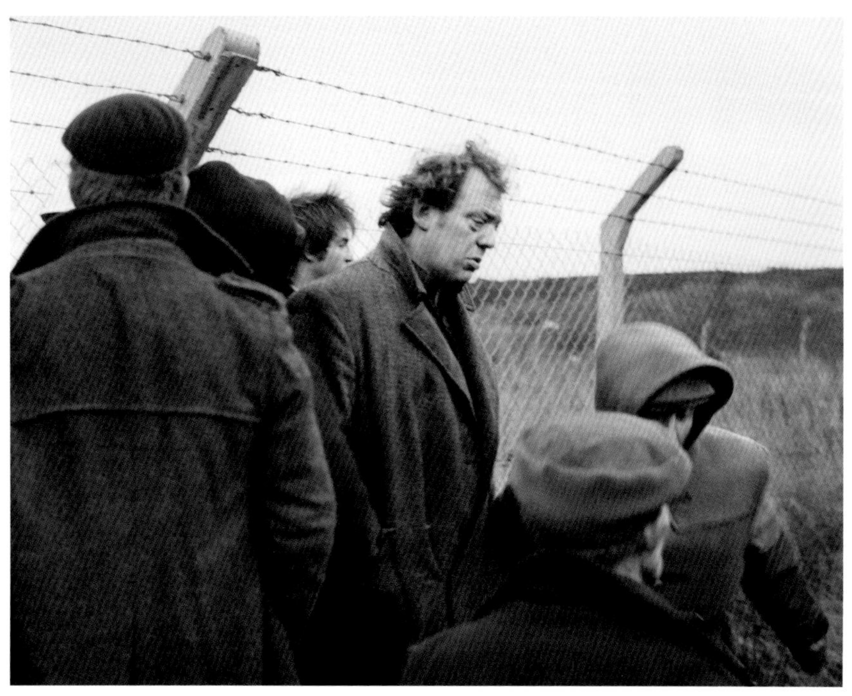

  Brian at the disputed fence 1983

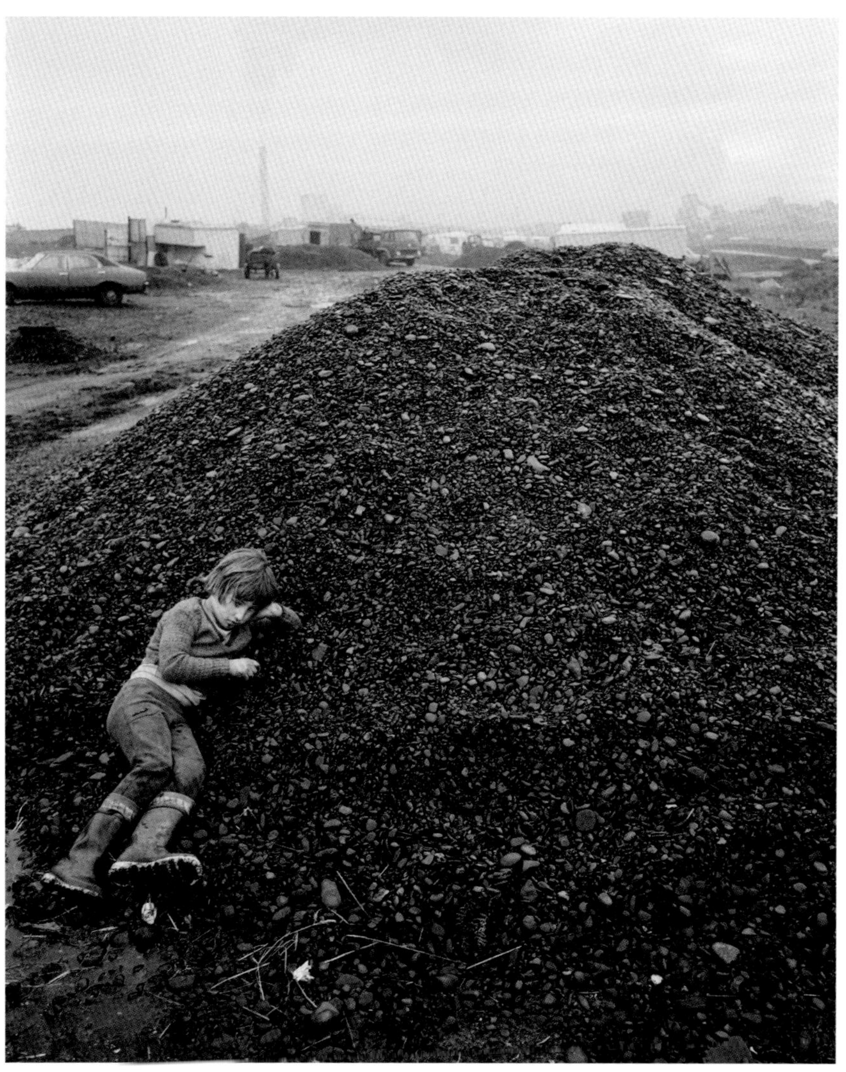

  Johnny at the Coal, Seacoal Camp 1983

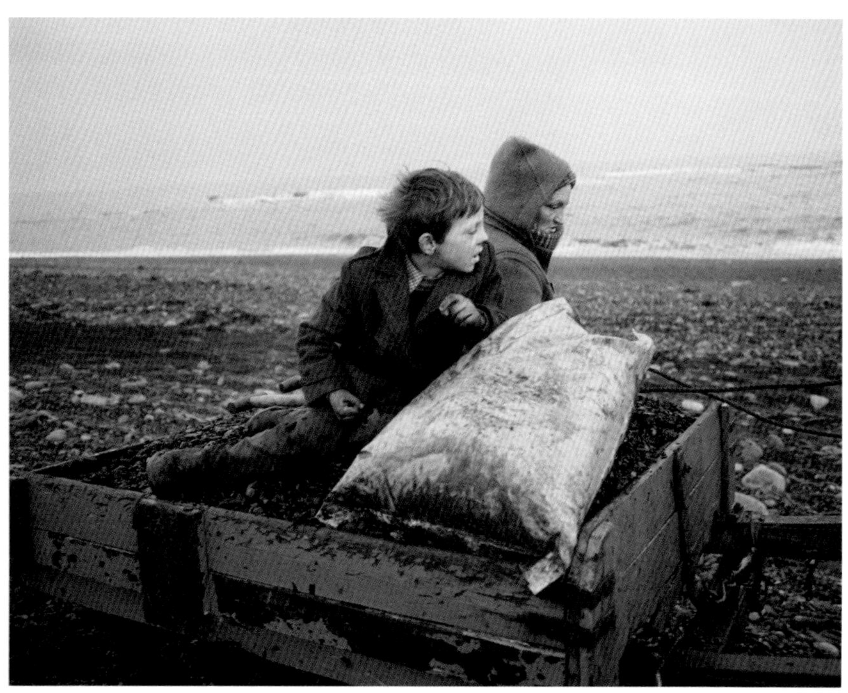

   Rocker and Rosie going home 1983

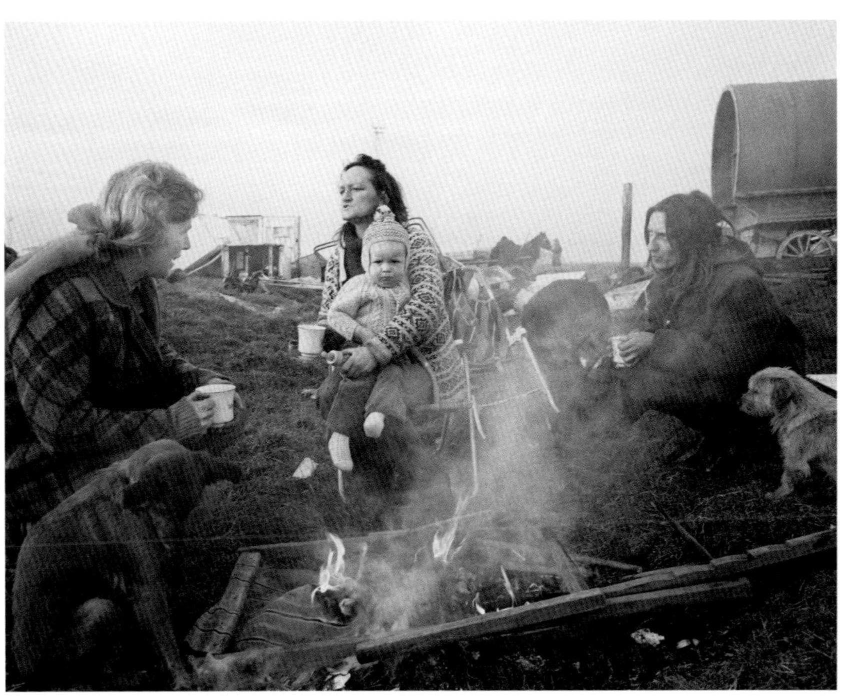

  Margaret, Rosie, and Val 1983

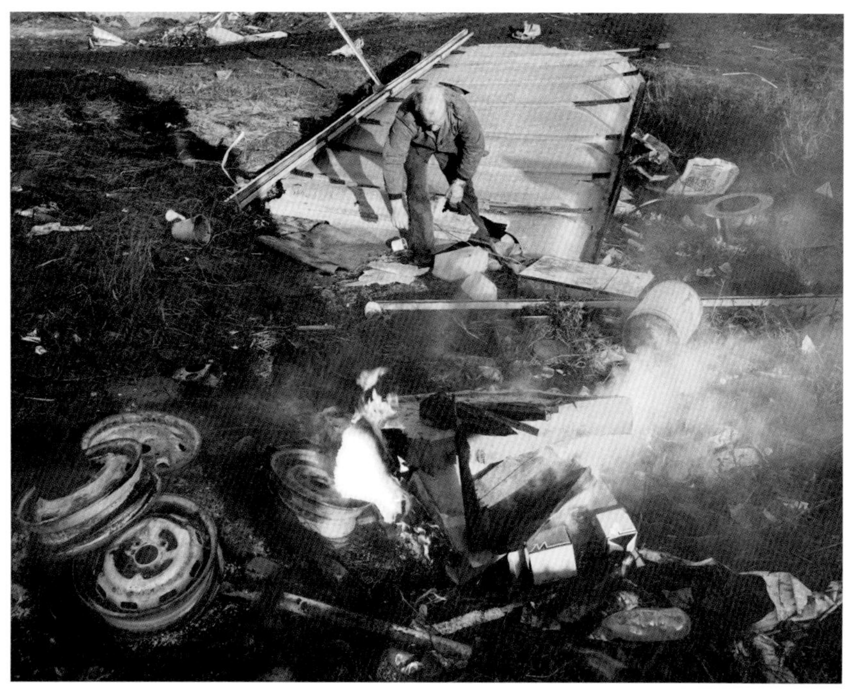

38   *Collie burning rubbish* 1983

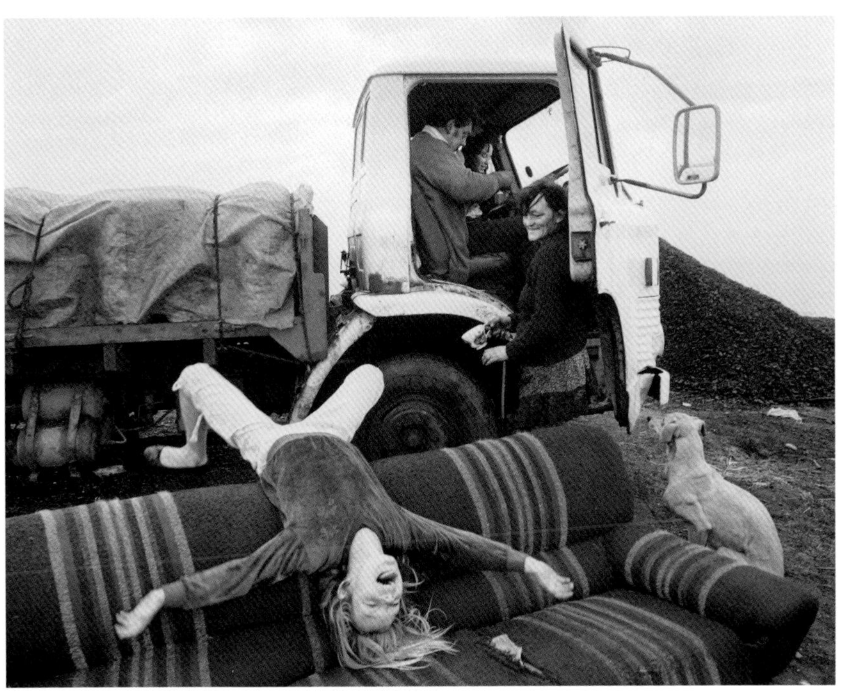

 Helen Laidler with her parents Rosie and Brian and her sister Alison 1983

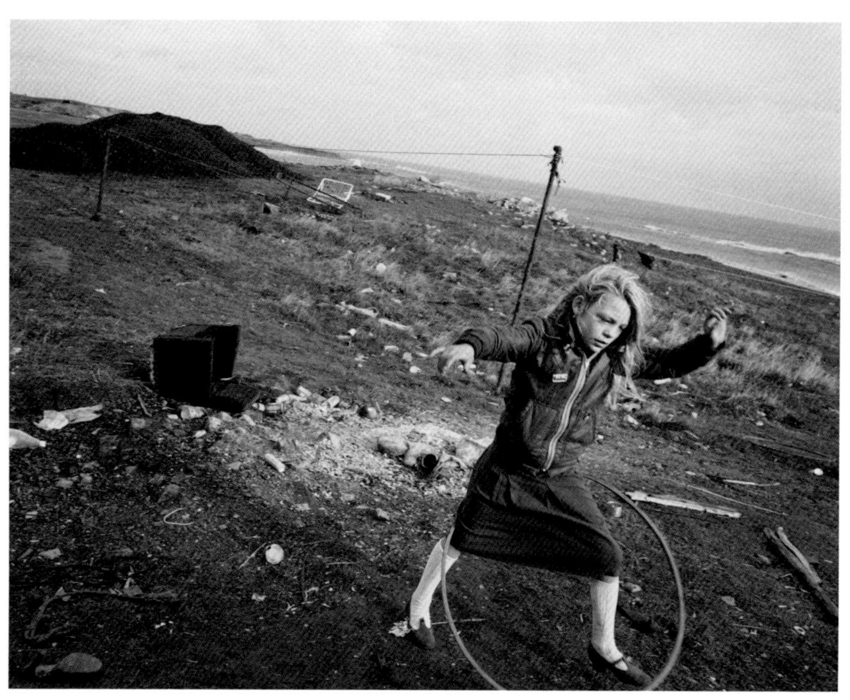

40   *Helen and her Hula-Hoop, Seacoal Camp* 1983

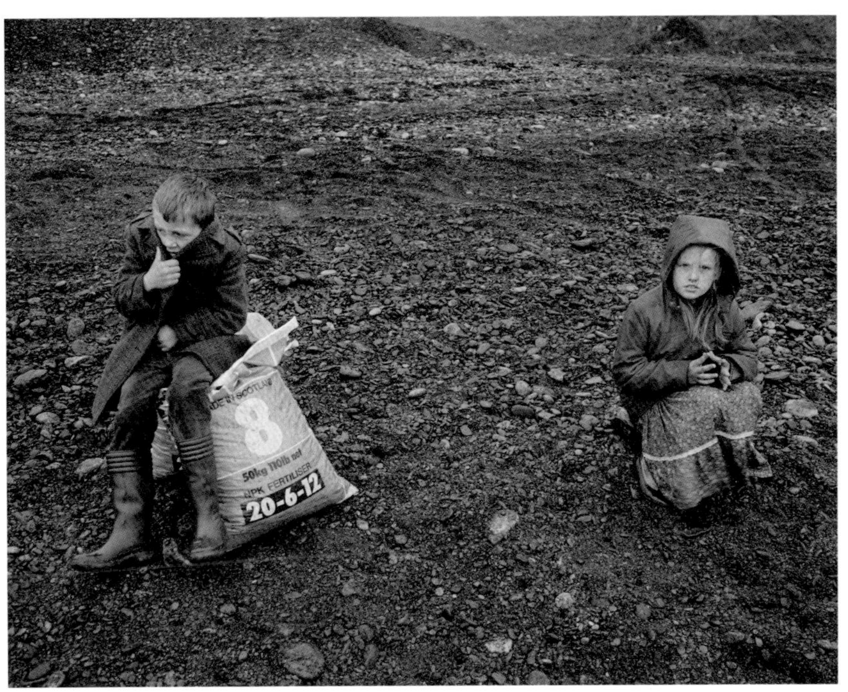

     Rocker and Claire 1983

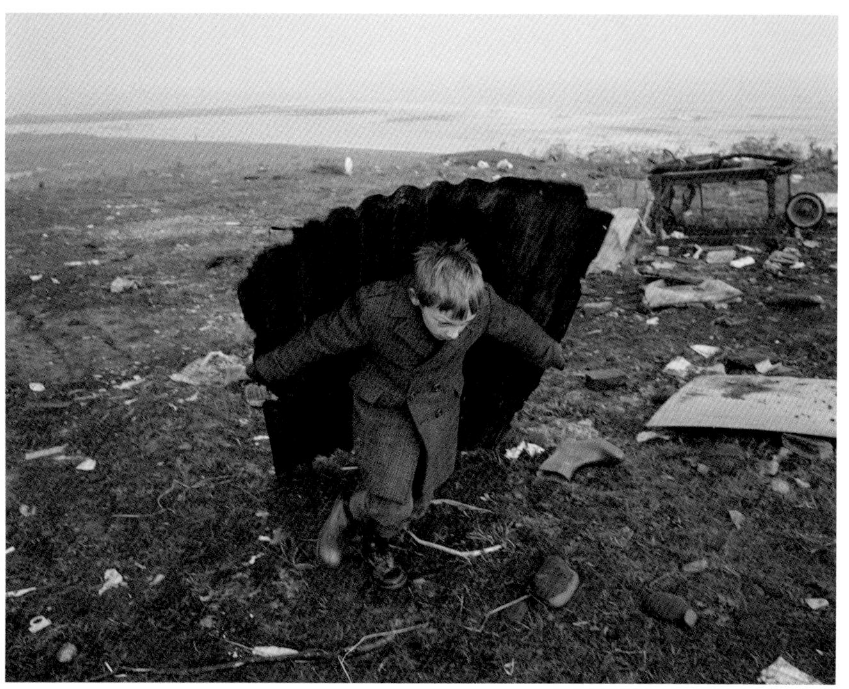

    Rocker collecting steel for money, Seacoal Camp 1982

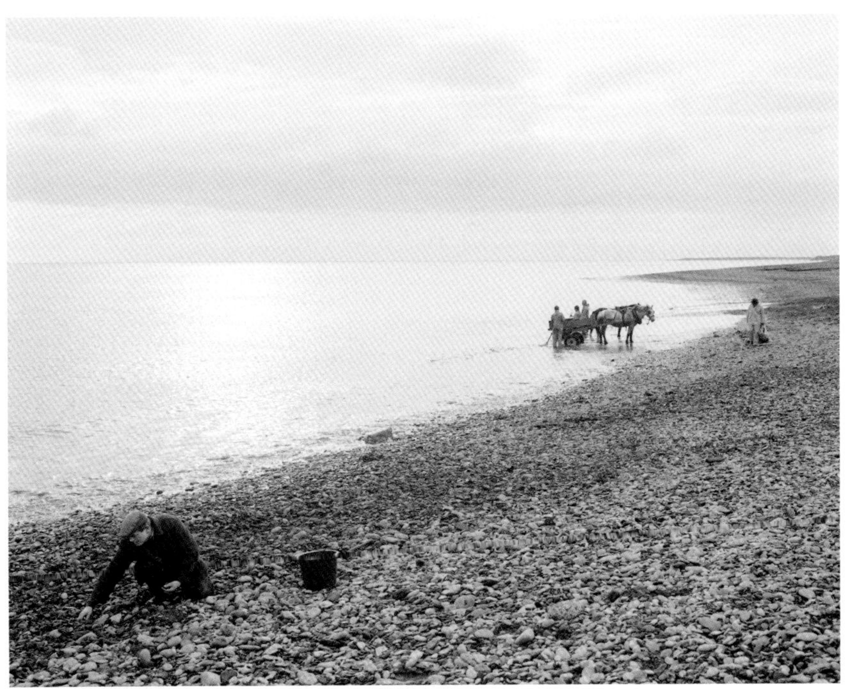

  Hand Picker, Seacoal Beach 1983

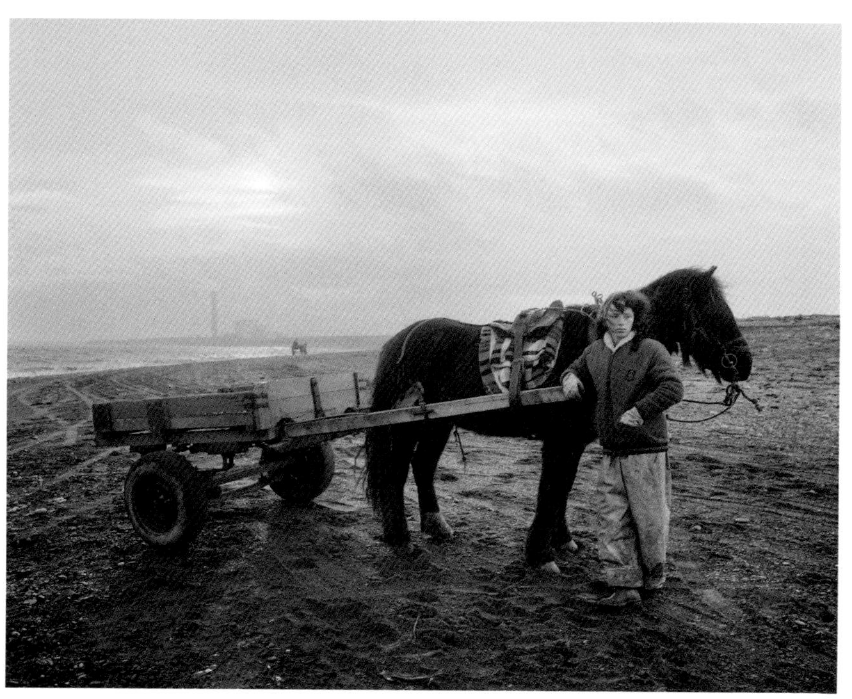

    Alison at the Beach 1983

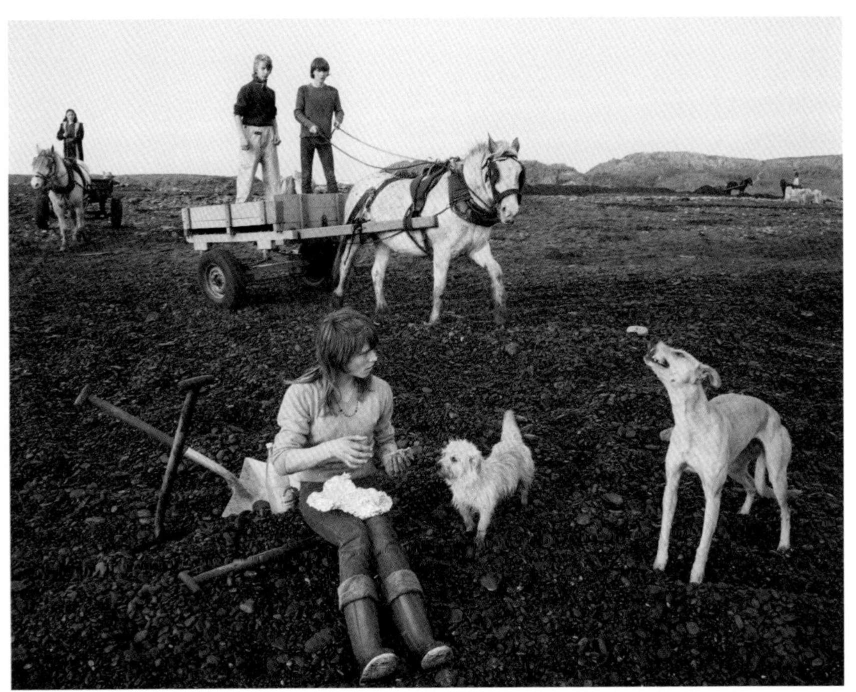

45 *Nini having lunch* 1983

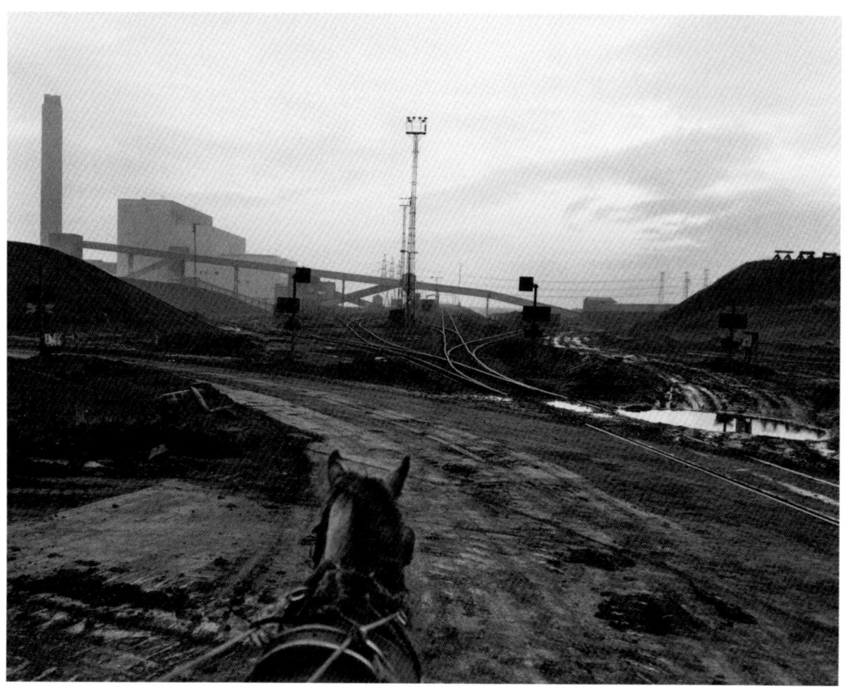

 At Meagol Ride through Lynemouth Pit 1982

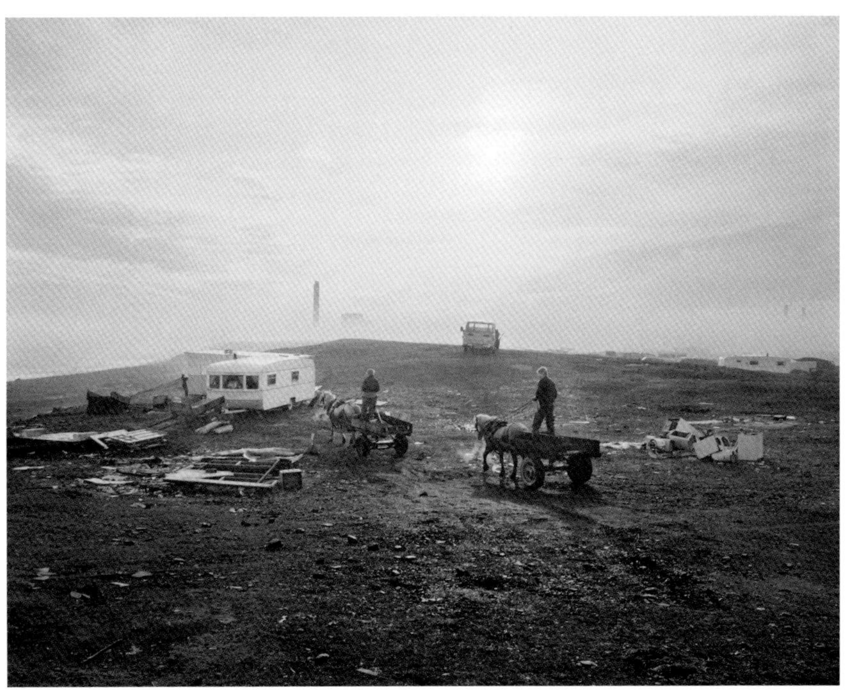

    Seacoal Camp, Lynemouth 1983

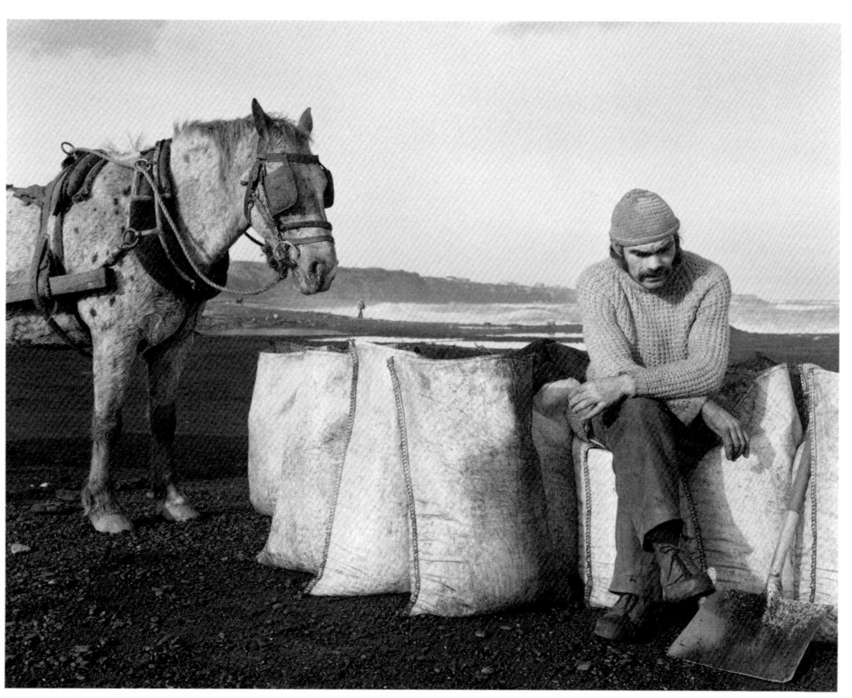

   Man resting and spotted horse, Seacoal Beach 1984

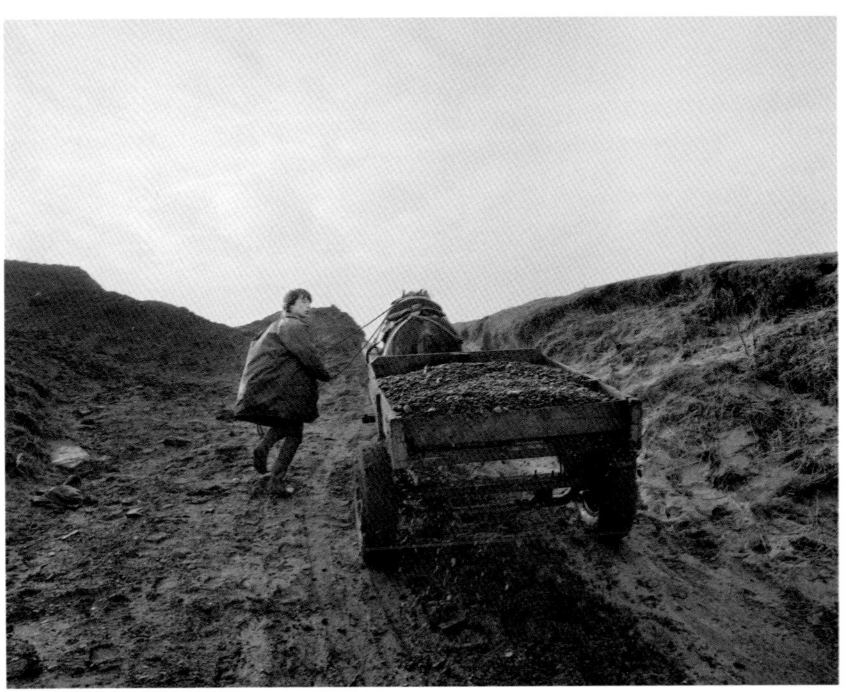

    Nini leaving the beach, Seacoal Beach 1983

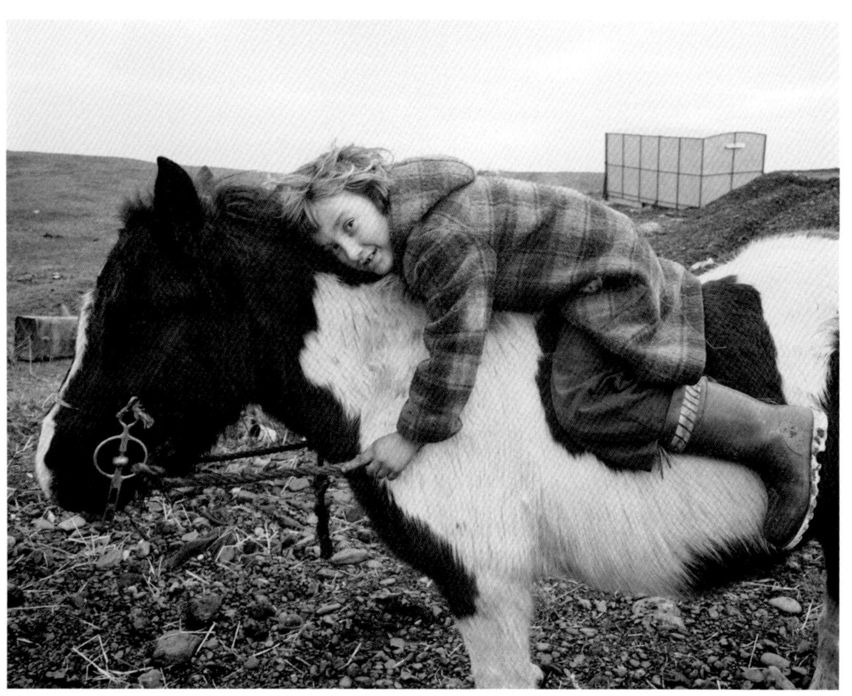

     John and a horse 1984

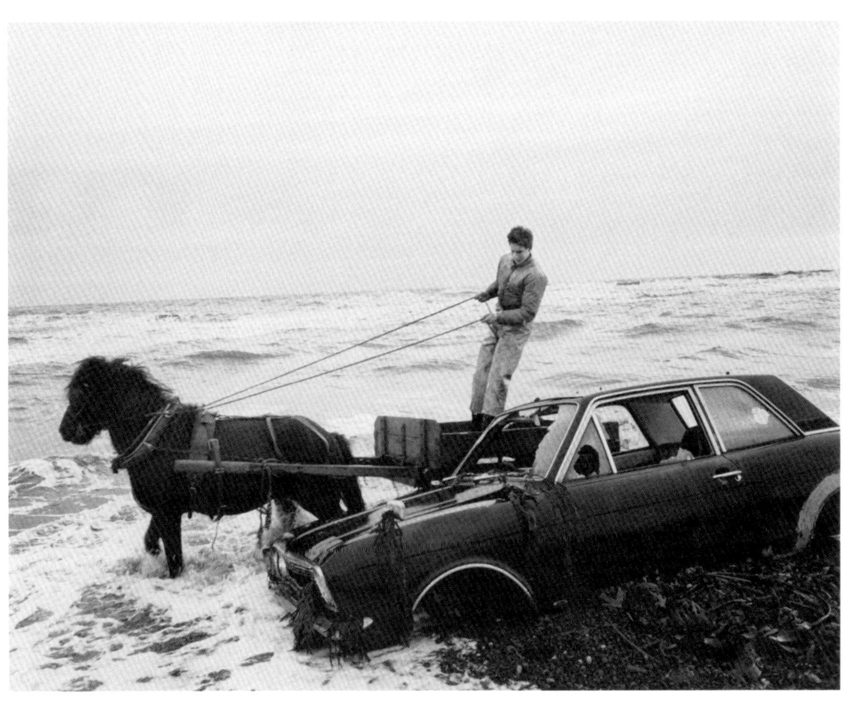

  Seacoal Beach 1983

SKINNINGROVE

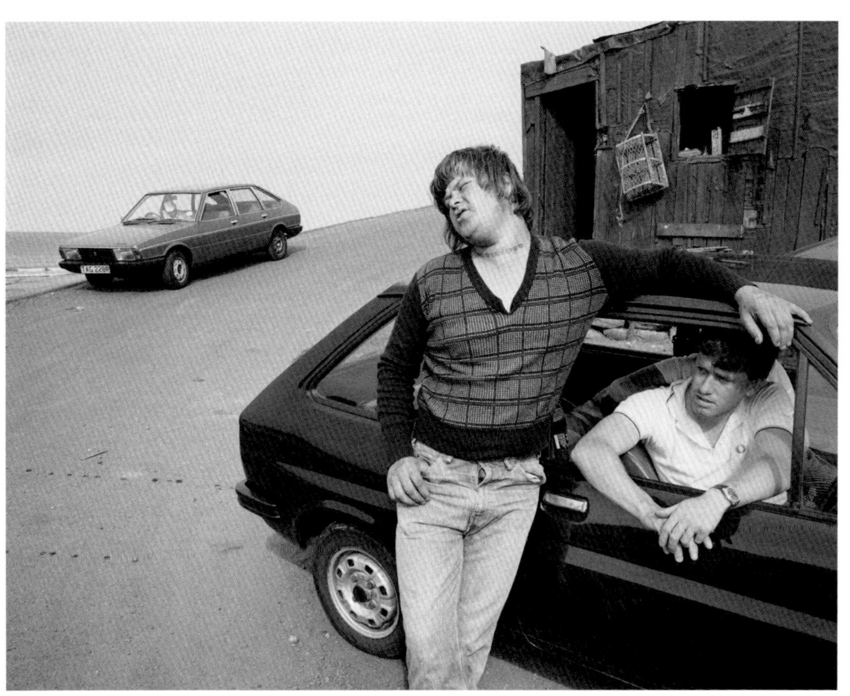

   Bever taking in the morning sun 1982

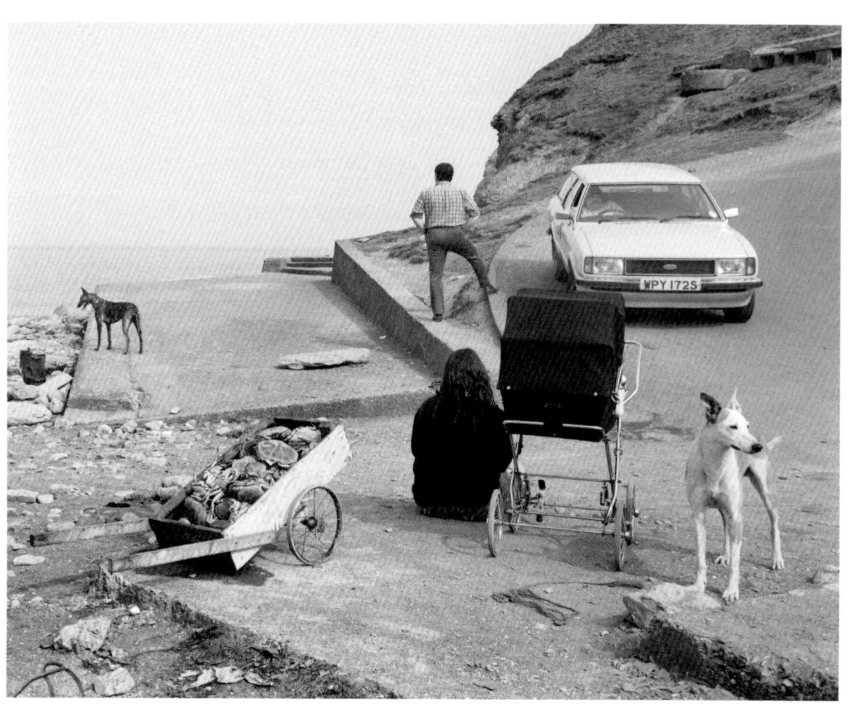

    Crabs, people, dogs 1981

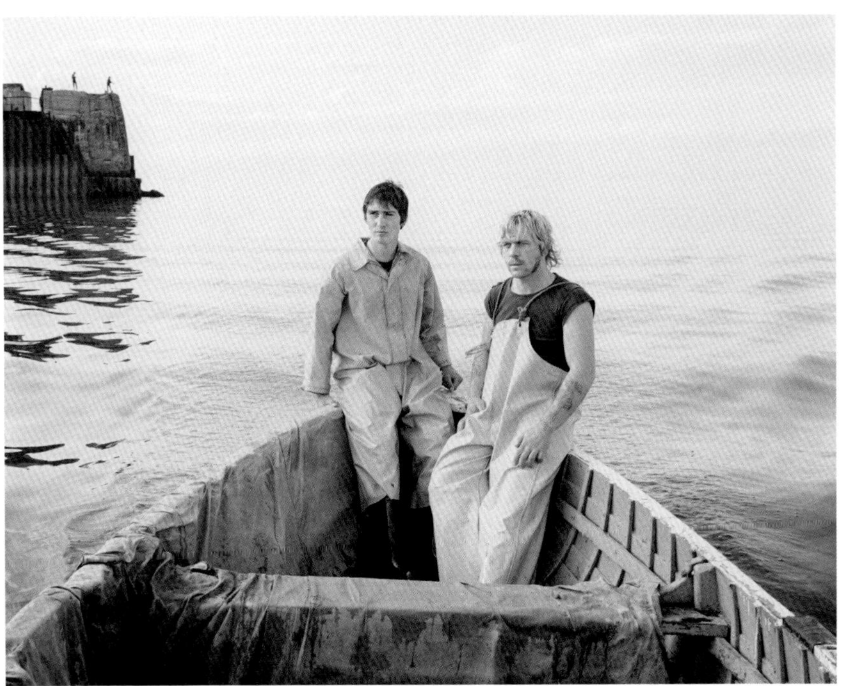

55   *Blackie and Matty* 1982

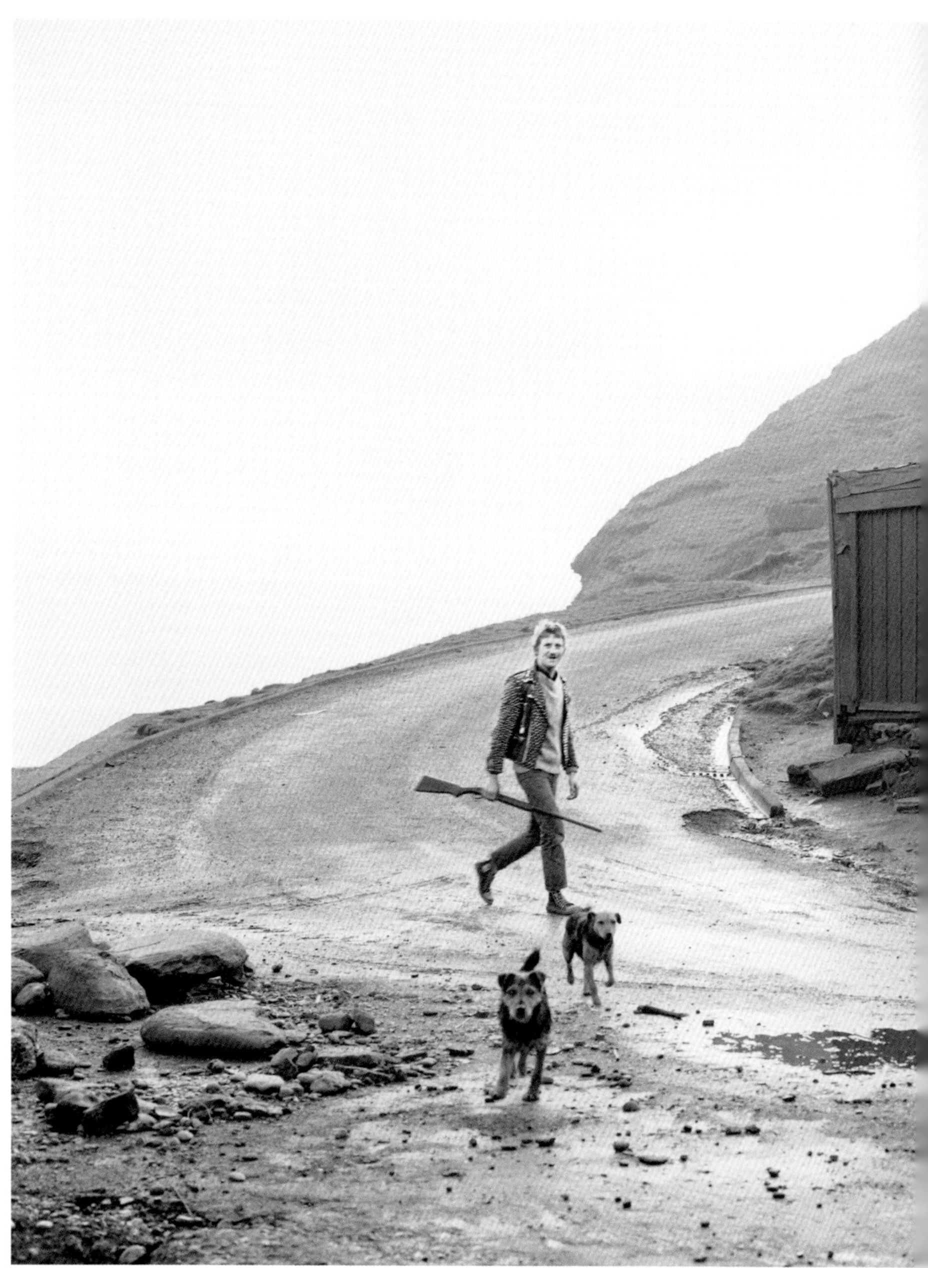

  Leso with his dogs and a gun, Skinningrove 1983

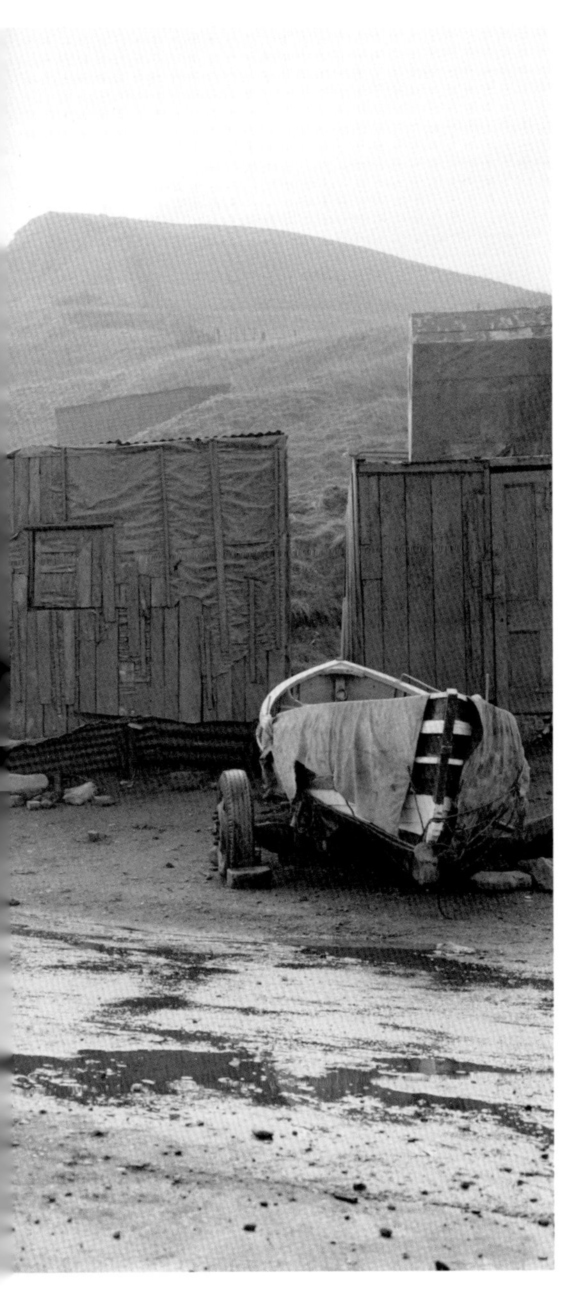

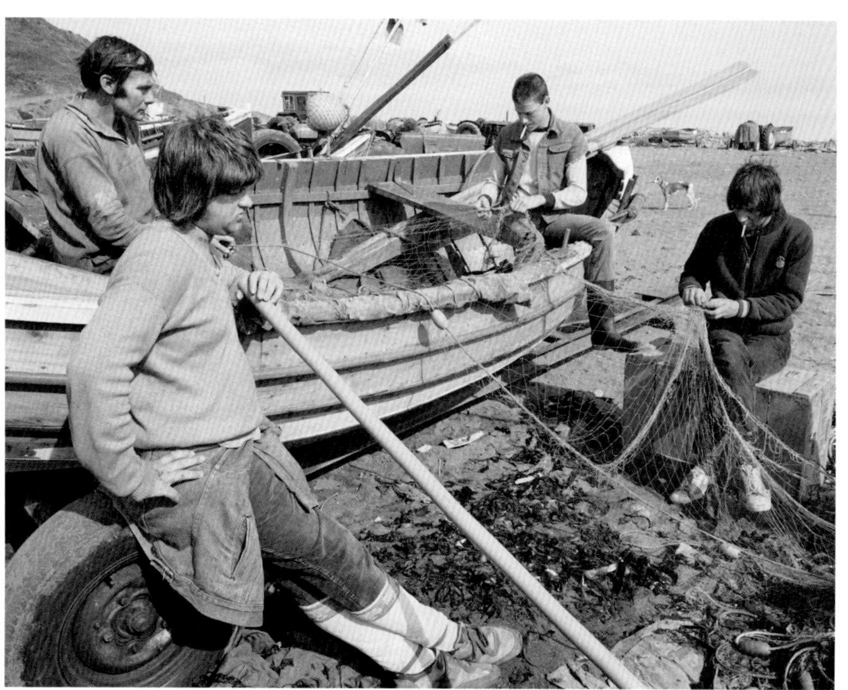

   Brian McCabe, Bever, unidentified youth and Toothie cleaning nets 1983

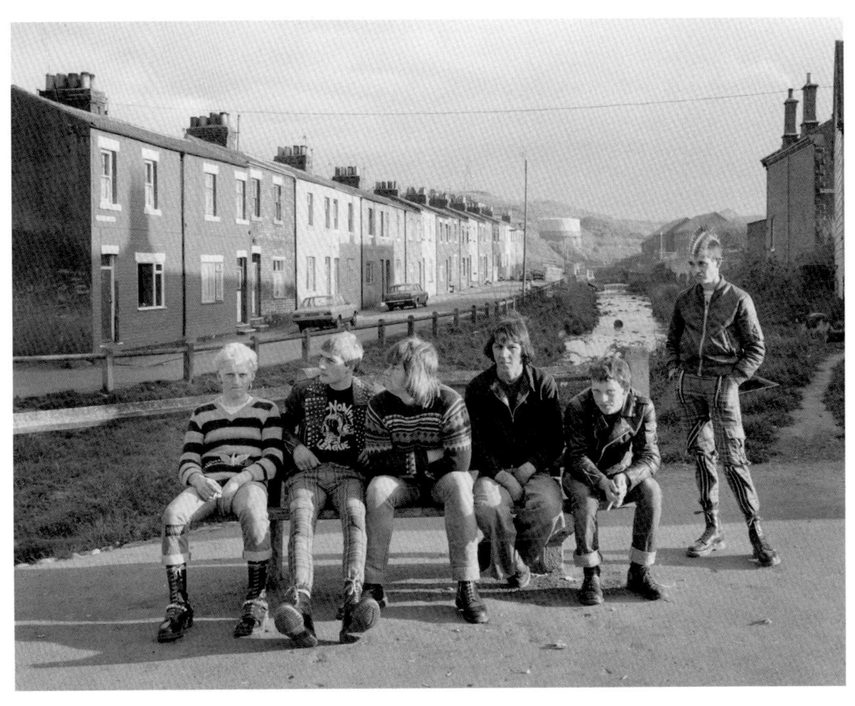

Leso (Leslie Holliday), Blackie (Terrance Whitney), Bever (Trevor McConnell), Toothie (Steve Tooth), Richard (Richard Noble), and Whippet (Malcolm Whitney) 1982

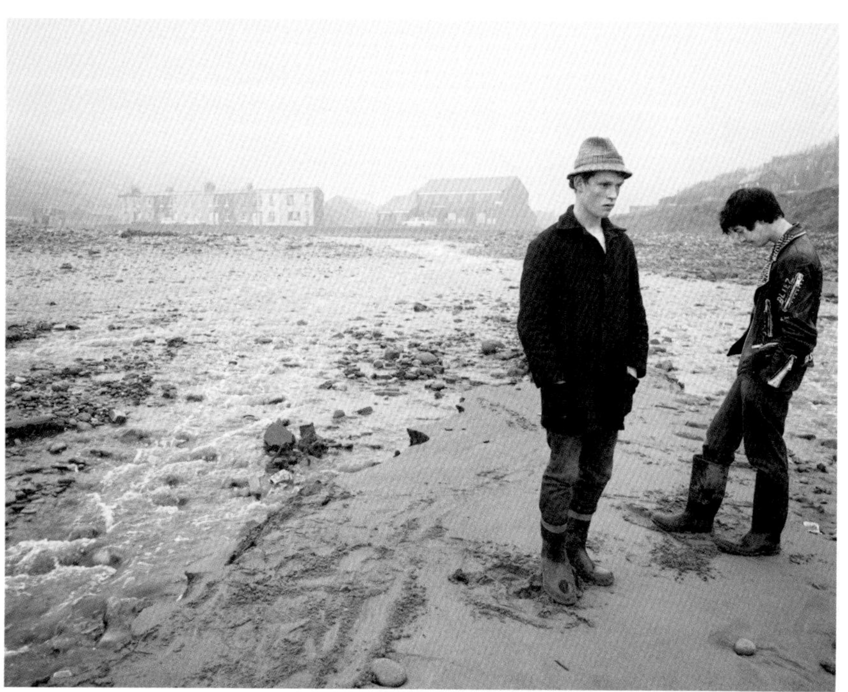

   Richard and Whippet waiting by the beck 1983

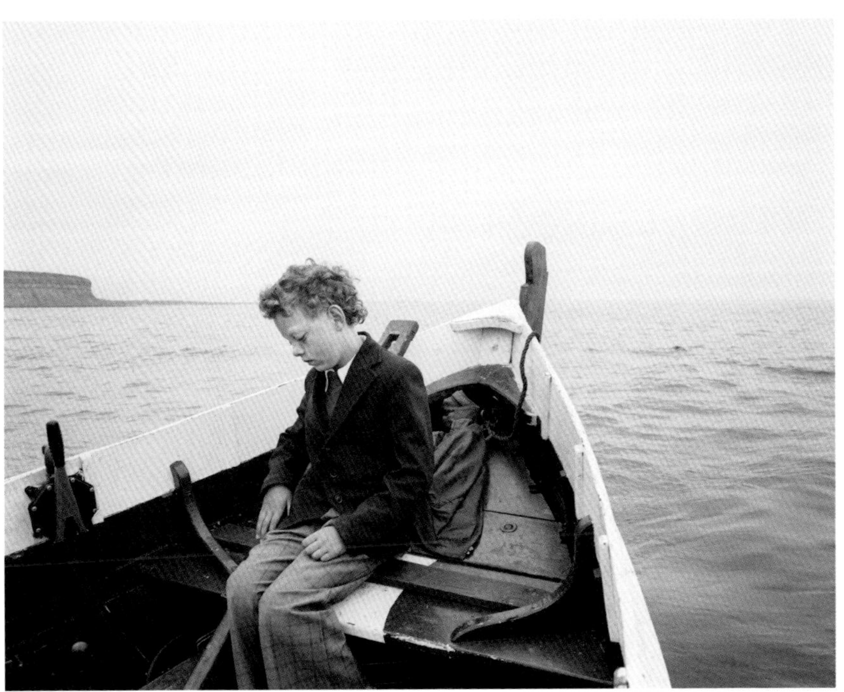

 Simon Coultas being taken to sea for the first time since his father David drowned 1984

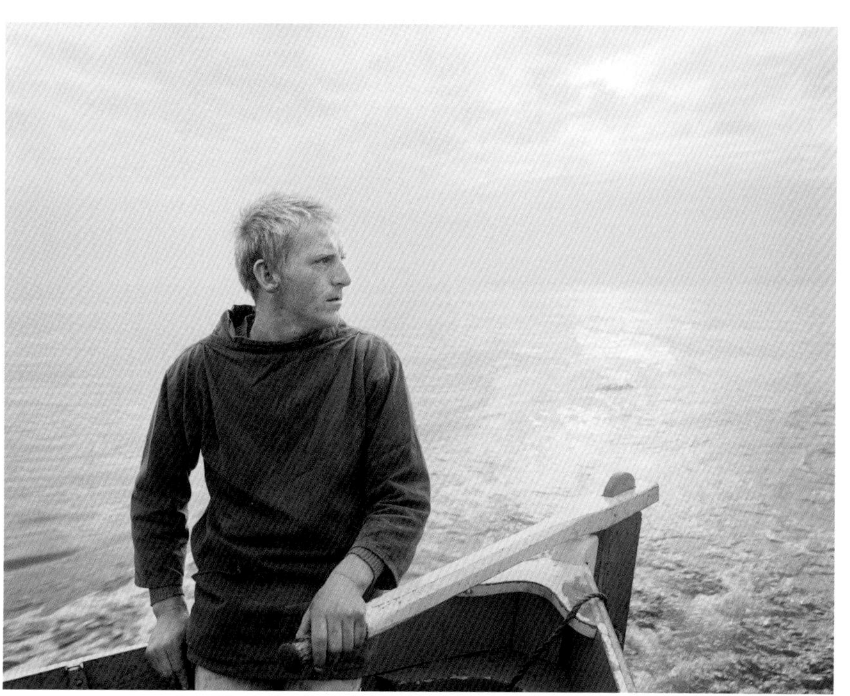

  Leso at sea, Skinningrove 1983

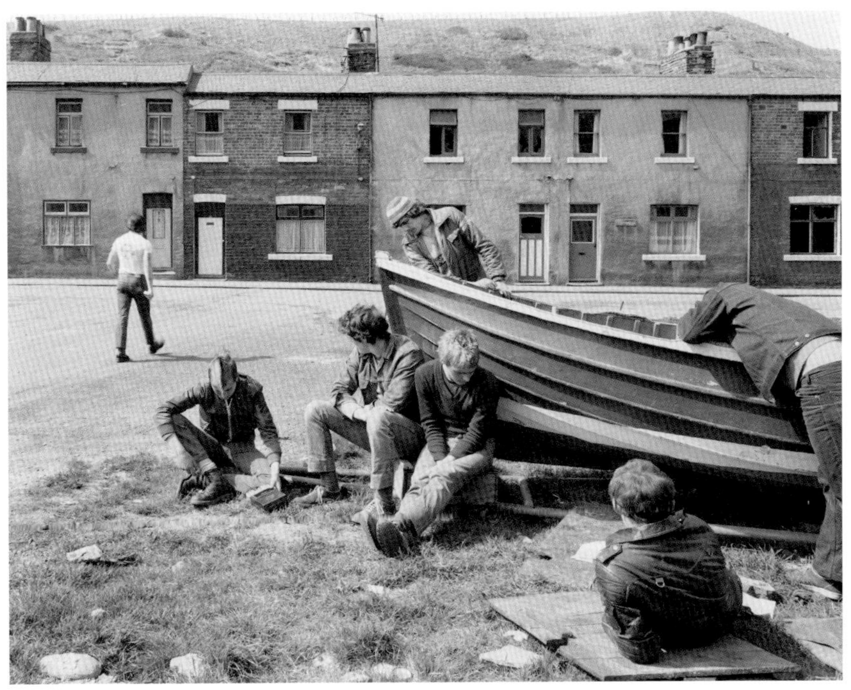

63   *Boat repairs* 1982